GW01395968

THE TECHNIQUE OF ADVOCACY

THE TECHNIQUE OF ADVOCACY

by
John Munkman LLB
*of the Middle Temple and North-eastern Circuit,
Barrister-at-Law*

With foreword by
Gilbert Gray QC

Butterworths
London, Dublin and Edinburgh
1991

United Kingdom	Butterworth & Co (Publishers) Ltd, 88 Kingsway, LONDON WC2B 6AB and 4 Hill Street, EDINBURGH EH2 3JZ
Australia	Butterworths Pty Ltd, SYDNEY, MELBOURNE, BRISBANE, ADELAIDE, PERTH, CANBERRA and HOBART
Canada	Butterworths Canada Ltd, TORONTO and VANCOUVER
Ireland	Butterworth (Ireland) Ltd, DUBLIN
Malaysia	Malayan Law Journal Sdn Bhd, KUALA LUMPUR
New Zealand	Butterworths of New Zealand Ltd, WELLINGTON and AUCKLAND
Puerto Rico	Equity de Puerto Rico, Inc, HATO REY
Singapore	Malayan Law Journal Pte Ltd, SINGAPORE
USA	Butterworth Legal Publishers, AUSTIN, Texas; BOSTON, Massachusetts; CLEARWATER, Florida (D & S Publishers); ORFORD, New Hampshire (Equity Publishing); ST PAUL, Minnesota; and SEATTLE, Washington

All rights reserved. No part of this publication may be reproduced in any material form (including photocopying or storing it in any medium by electronic means and whether or not transiently or incidentally to some other use of this publication) without the written permission of the copyright owner except in accordance with the provisions of the Copyright, Designs and Patents Act 1988 or under the terms of a licence issued by the Copyright Licensing Agency Ltd, 90 Tottenham Court Road, London, England W1P 9HE. Applications for the copyright owner's written permission to reproduce any part of this publication should be addressed to the publisher.

Warning : The doing of an unauthorised act in relation to a copyright work may result in both a civil claim for damages and criminal prosecution.

© Butterworth & Co (Publishers) Ltd 1991

A CIP Catalogue record for this book is available from the British Library.

ISBN   0 406 00264 9

Printed and bound by Bookcraft (Bath) Ltd, Midsomer Norton, Avon

Foreword

by Gilbert Gray, QC

Most books on advocacy are unreadable. They should be regarded as a warning, not as an example. Many who write on the subject should never speak on it. Some who do both would be well advised to do neither.

Advocacy is the art of persuasion. It is also a craft. As in music, there are rules, without which discord follows. John Munkman has observed the rules and written a masterpiece.

This book is a treasure. Tuition merges into intuition. His acute analysis and logical development is scholarly, scientific and succinct. It is like first looking into Chapman's *Homer*.

John Munkman has a laser beam eye. Sharp intellect (not ancient anecdote) develops and adorns the theme of this book. He clarifies where others cloud. He distills where others dilute.

His other books on *Damages for Personal Injuries and Death* and *Employer's Liability* are superb. So is this volume.

All advocates like to look back and relish moments of adversarial glory. John Munkman enables us to see why such moments were glorious, and how they might have been better. Mutatis mutandis, he does the same for our many more numerous calamities also.

This is one of those rare books where the messenger never gets in the way of the message. The message is lucid and the style deceptively simple. It is a joy to read, and enlightenment shines from every page. It is a classic.

Gilbert Gray, QC

Preface

I wrote this book many years ago when I was trying to discover the techniques of advocacy for myself, especially how to ask questions, because although there were many books with hints and anecdotes, no one had explored the subject scientifically. Many of the key ideas about things which I found puzzling were evolved in odd moments in the Burma frontier hills during the Japanese war.

The first edition had a wide circulation. Substantial parts were translated into Norwegian as part of a manual for the Norwegian Bar. Large parts were also used in a book by an Indian judge, and extracts were used by a Canadian author. Nevertheless I have felt some diffidence about re-issuing it, because in 1961, as I was beginning to have some success, I was compelled by prolonged illness in the family to give up advocacy, and have since practised as a legal adviser only. However, there has been such a persistent stream of letters demanding copies from all parts of the world — Adelaide, Greece, Zimbabwe, Kuala Lumpur in the last few weeks — , that it seems right to re-issue it.

The text is substantially unaltered, although I have made revisions where necessary, for instance to quote the 1990 Code of Conduct for the English Bar. The subject does not change. More up-to-date examples could perhaps have been introduced, but this would have involved a prolonged search of numerous transcripts which are not easy to get: also to rake over the embers of recent trials may cause distress to those involved, especially in some cases where the scandal attached to their name has now been forgotten. But I have added a new chapter on 'Learning the Techniques of Advocacy' which also serves to recapitulate the main points of the book.

There is one thing to which, in retrospect, I would not have attached the same importance, and I have toned it down in the text to some extent. This is what I called 'Massive Confrontation', exemplified particularly by the famous libel cases such as the Oscar Wilde case where every awkward detail of a person's past life is brought up against him. The truth is that these cases owe everything to the skill of the solicitors and inquiry agents who have amassed all the evidence, and less than is claimed to the advocates such as Carson who made use of it, though of course it requires great skill to select what is most important out of a great mass of material and marshal it in the most effective order. The only difference between these cases and the everyday technique which I have called 'firm insinuation' is a difference of scale.

The preliminary sketches for the book were published as a series of articles in that excellent magazine, *Law Notes*, which also published the substance of the new chapter in December 1988.

I have to thank my old friend Gilbert Gray, QC, for contributing a foreword, which I invited him to do to overcome my diffidence about reissuing the book. He is one of the most colourful advocates of the present day, with a jovial, friendly presence which lights up dull moments and disarms opposition, but hides a quick turn of thought and an equally quick turn of phrase, effective in both argument and cross-examination.

John Munkman

Contents

Chapter 1

Advocacy: Its Nature, Aims and Background

1 Meaning and foundations

In its widest sense, advocacy is the art of convincing others, that is to say the *art of persuasion*. In this general sense it is a valued accomplishment in many departments of life — such as commerce and finance, labour relations and politics — as well as in law.

Here, however, we are concerned with the specialised meaning of the word as used by lawyers: and in its legal context, advocacy is the art of conducting cases in court, both by argument and by the manner of bringing out the evidence, so as to convince the court or jury, as the case may be.

For members of the bar, and for those solicitors who make a practice of appearing in court, advocacy is of the first importance and ranks at any rate on an equal level with a knowledge of the law. For other solicitors its importance is perhaps less evident, but they also must have some knowledge of the subject, partly because they prepare the material for use in court, partly because they have to assess the special aptitudes of the counsel they engage from time to time. Moreover, it is frequently necessary in the course of everyday practice to convince others and to ask searching questions, and this is a informal exercise of the same arts which, on a more developed plane, are used in the courts.

Inadequate treatment of the subject

It is surprising, in the light of the key position of advocacy, that it has taken so long for it to be explained and analysed in a systematic fashion. In 1951, when this book was first published, there was no text-book on the subject and it had no place in the Law Schools or in professional examinations. There were a few small books, mostly originating in the United States, which gave hints and anecdotes, but these, even allowing for their limited scope, were decidedly old-fashioned. They told us about such things as warranties on the sale of horses and the occupational dishonesty of horse dealers, and about old time advocates so overpowering that, in the presence of those piercing eyes, no witness would dare to hide the truth. This brings back a memory of Stafford Cripps cross-examining (in a patent case about a radio valve) like a weasel with a rabbit, the only time I have seen that sort of dominance. But a reader of these books naturally felt unable to attain such magical powers, and fell back on rough hit-or-miss methods, learning in time from his mistakes. In recent years the situation has changed. The professional organisations are running courses on advocacy and there are several modern text books, though the emphasis of both courses and books tends to be on court procedure and etiquette rather than technique.[1]

Sources of knowledge

Nevertheless, much of the technique of advocacy can be discovered and explained. A great mass of material is

---

[1]   Marcus Stone, Cross-examination in Criminal Trials (Butterworths 1988) goes into considerable detail, but it is largely about tactics in criminal cases taken as a whole rather than the technique of asking questions.

available, and the best approach is by analysing the methods of such leaders as John Simon and Norman Birkett, who have set the style for our times, rather than by looking back to remote and old-fashioned figures such as Abraham Lincoln and James Scarlett. The sources of knowledge about advocacy consist mainly of the standard biographies of outstanding lawyers and verbatim reports of important trials: but a word of caution is necessary in dealing with each of these sources. Biographers nearly always tend to show exaggerated hero-worship, and it is necessary to allow for this tendency: legends grow up round distinguished men in civilised societies, just as they grew up round the Homeric heroes at the dawn of history. In fact, of course, the greatest figures have had their mistakes and failures, though these are often suppressed in their biographies. Another point is that biographers are not particularly interested in explaining the technical approach to a difficult cross-examination, for example, and are more ready to give up space to a clever retort which, however striking, is devoid of technical value.

As to published reports of trials, these are of great value if distinguished advocates appeared, since they illustrate the exercise of the technique of advocacy in its most polished form. In these important cases, however, the high standard of performance is greatly helped by the care taken to amass useful material, and the issues are often of an unusual kind.

Naturally observation of the conduct of everyday cases is another leading source of knowledge; here the beginner's difficulty is that he does not always know whether the case is being conducted well or indifferently.

The aim of this book is to extract from these varied sources some of the general principles governing the technique of advocacy, chiefly for the assistance of the beginner, though a knowledge of these principles may help even accomplished advocates to handle their technique more consciously and effectively; but it should be realised that the subject is both large and difficult, and that deeper research will be needed to give anything like a complete picture.

Advocacy as an art

Advocacy is not a science, like law, but an art, and therefore, to a greater extent, it is a highly individual attainment. Like every other art – and like a knowledge of law, for that matter – it cannot be developed without some initial aptitude, and it cannot be mastered without practical experience of handling cases. On the other hand, again like every other art, it does not depend on aptitude and experience alone, but has its rules in technique. These rules of technique can be explained and learnt. They are like the principle of perspective and the use of colours in painting, or scales and arpeggios in music, or the making of incisions and the insertion of stitches in surgery.

The difference between the science of law and the art of advocacy can be stated quite simply. So far as law is concerned, once its principles are known and understood, there is an end of the matter. To know the technique of advocacy, however, is only the starting point: it has to be handled and used in varied circumstances and according to one's own individual style.

Qualities needed by an advocate

As already stated, some initial aptitude is needed in order to become an advocate. The qualities which seem to be required by a competent advocate are summarised below. It will be noted that most of these can be developed by the average educated man, if he does not possess them already .

(1) A good voice

It does not need to be a very loud voice, since the carrying power of a voice depends on its quality rather than its volume, but it is necessary to be able to speak clearly and distinctly. A monotonous voice will soon tire both the judge and the jury, so that some variation of tone is also important. Voice development and elocution are naturally outside the scope of this book. Nevertheless, one practical point may be stressed: in speaking in court it is best to go fairly slowly, as otherwise part of the argument may be missed.

(2) Command of words

A sound command of the English language is another essential. Without this it is impossible to frame questions readily in cross-examination, to frame non-leading questions in examination-in-chief, or to deliver speeches at short notice. An accurate and varied style needs much cultivation. The essentials of style in court are simplicity and clearness: if it is possible, in addition, to be interesting, and occasionally picturesque, especially in addressing a jury, so much the better.

(3) Confidence

No quality carries an advocate further than this: it played an incalculable part, for instance, in the success of the first Earl of Birkenhead, even allowing for his brilliance in other directions. Confidence can be cultivated. The confident handling of a case, once it has started, is in no way inconsistent with a certain nervous tension beforehand, such as athletes feel before starting a race, but every effort should be made to eliminate this feeling. The ideal state, as for an athlete, is one of alert relaxation.

(4) Persistence

Persistence is a marked characteristic of the average successful advocate: it enables him to fight cases to the end in spite of unexpected difficulties, and is a most valuable asset in cross-examining.

(5) Practical judgment

This needs a little explanation. Knowledge of law, and of technique, is a knowledge of general principles. The nearer one gets to individual facts, the less one is guided by general principles, and the more by the *feel* of things: this ability to judge individual situations may to some extent be innate, but it is generally acquired by experience, and it is convenient to call it practical judgment. It is exemplified by the ability to scent a weak point when cross-examining, or in the selection of the central issue on which a case is fought, or in judging probabilities, and indeed in many other connections.

(6) Experience of handling cases

It is not enough to know the rules of technique, it is necessary also to have practice in handling them. To give an example from another branch of knowledge, a student of algebra may understand perfectly well that x can be used to represent an unknown quantity, but he will probably make mistakes in handling it until he has had some practice. Nevertheless, knowledge of the rules of technique is a first-class starting point, infinitely superior to the hit-or-miss approach resting on experience alone.

The last two qualities, it will be noticed, are acquired by experience: and it is in these respects, in gaining practical judgment and an ability to handle cases without clumsy mistakes that one 'learns by experience'. It might be added that experience does not always teach: there are plenty who have had years of experience, but learnt very little.

Background knowledge

Knowledge of all kinds of things is useful to an advocate, but there are certain subjects which are of outstanding value. These include the following:

(1) The law of evidence and procedure

Though his knowledge of the substantive law may be vague, an advocate must have the rules of evidence at his finger-tips, and to a lesser extent — so far as concerns procedure in court — he must be familiar with the rules of procedure. Subjects of special practical importance are the limits of the hearsay rule, admissions, confessions, evidence of similar facts, and the proof of documents (including notices to produce and to admit): and, in connection with procedure, the order of speeches, the rules governing the examination of witnesses, and the orders which may be made by the court as to the payment of costs.

(2) Professional ethics

There are various rules which have been settled by the legal profession to govern the conduct of advocates in such matters as attacking the character of a witness. Some of these rules are referred to later.

(3) Logic

A knowledge of logic is not indispensable, but there are times when an elementary knowledge of the subject can be helpful. In particular it is useful to be able to pick out fallacies of reasoning. There is a well-known example in the question:

'When did you stop beating your wife? Answer Yes or No.'

This is the fallacy of Many Questions which combines several questions into one and assumes that one of them has been answered in a certain way. Of course, everyone would recognise the fallacy in this particular example, but it may appear in more subtle forms. Again, arguments are often presented in the form:

'Either this is the case, or that is the case.'

Such arguments are not conclusive unless the alternatives exhaust all the possibilities, and an advocate who has an elementary knowledge of logic will be quick to point out the omission of other possible explanations.

In an argument on legal principle, an accurate logician has a marked advantage, not only in close reasoning but also in ability to distinguish and classify cases, and in ability to frame definitions and express propositions of law with great precision.

However, the value of logic to a lawyer must not be overrated: an elementary knowledge will go a long way.

(4) Knowledge of mankind and of affairs

Advocacy, like teaching and medicine, is an art which co-operates with human nature, because it works on the minds of the judge, the jury and the witnesses. Besides, the facts in most cases are concerned in part, at any rate, with the actions of the parties and of other persons, and motives and probabilities play a leading part in legal argument on the facts, unless these are proved conclusively by direct evidence. For these reasons a knowledge of ordinary human behaviour and of the springs of human action is fundamental.

Likewise, the law touches on most branches of human affairs in one form or another, and a superficial acquaintance with almost any topic may facilitate the presentation of a case. Of the many things with which the law is concerned, some arise with great frequency, and it is useful to know something about the habits and living conditions of all social grades (valuable in divorce and criminal practice), about elementary anatomy, about commercial accounts, and about the working of machines[2].

[2]   Marshall Hall's deep knowledge of firearms, poisons and jewellery was of immense value to him as the greatest of modern defending advocates in criminal trials: see his *Life*, by Edward Marjoribanks (1929), *passim*.

General knowledge of this kind cannot, of course, be cultivated all at once, but is gradually added to, little by little, in the course of practice.

(5) General principles of law

It would not be necessary to include this heading, but for the fact that it is often said that a good advocate need not be a good lawyer — sometimes with the corollary that a good lawyer cannot be a good advocate. It is true that questions of law do not often arise in everyday practice, and that most trials turn entirely on the facts. All the same, other things being equal, an advocate who is also a good lawyer — and does not obtrude his law until it is necessary — has an advantage over an advocate who is not. What is required is a firm grasp of *principle*: if at the same time a leading case can be quoted at random to support the principle, so much the better, but no one attempts to remember all the detailed refinements of case law.

That knowledge of law and ability as an advocate are compatible is proved by the high average standard of the junior bar in both subjects. At a higher level, it is proved by the fact that many leading men have been at the same time brilliant lawyers and distinguished advocates: the examples of the Earl of Birkenhead and Viscount Simon at once spring to the mind.

2 The limits of advocacy

Practical limitations

The scope of advocacy depends on the case, and for this purpose all cases may conveniently be divided into three groups.

First of all there is the thoroughly bad case without any hope of success — just as there are some surgical operations which no surgeon would undertake, because he knows that failure is certain. Thus in some criminal cases there is direct evidence covering every loophole, and the only course available is to plead guilty and offer some considerations in mitigation. Likewise, on the civil side, no defence can be offered in the average debt-collecting action. It should not be rashly assumed, however, that a given case falls within this category. A very weak civil claim may have some scintilla of evidence to support it, and there is nearly always some defence, however thin, which can be raised in answer to a strong claim, at any rate in actions of tort. In a weak criminal case, if there is no positive defence, there may be some confusion in the evidence which can be accentuated sufficiently to raise a doubt in the minds of the jury. Notwithstanding these practical considerations, it should be realised that there are some cases so bad that the most brilliant counsel could not succeed.

At the other end of the scale are the cases which are so strong that, with proper handling, they cannot fail. These cases are not so common — at any rate, in civil actions — and they can be lost by careless preparation or by inadequate presentation. Good advocacy is therefore necessary even in strong cases. Criminal prosecutions, as a rule, are founded on strong evidence, yet the Crown is always careful in nominating prosecuting counsel.

The majority of civil actions, and a large proportion of criminal prosecutions, fall between the two extremes. It is in these uncertain cases that advocacy becomes a cardinal factor, and the cross-examination of the witnesses, or the speeches, or both, may turn the balance.

The proportion of cases where substantial points of law are raised is quite small, and it is better not to introduce questions of law unless it is absolutely necessary to do so.

Ethical limits of advocacy

Every party to a civil action, and every person charged with a criminal offence, is entitled to have his version of the case put before the court. It is no part of an advocate's duty to pre-judge the case: that is within the exclusive province of the jury, or the judge, as the case may be, after hearing both sides. Thus, counsel has no right to refuse a brief in a murder case, for instance, on the ground that he believes that the accused is guilty, and conversely, he must not allow himself to be so carried away by his personal belief in his client that he becomes a partisan instead of an advocate. In this personal capacity, an advocate should be detached from the case: in his capacity as an advocate, it is his duty to present the evidence and the arguments in favour of his client to the best of his ability, whether he believes in them or not. As a matter of fact, it becomes a habit to refrain from forming a decided opinion until the case is over.

There are some exceptions to these general principles. An advocate cannot allow himself to be made an instrument of fraud. For example, an advocate has no right to appear in an action to propound a will if he knows that the will has been forged. Likewise, it would be wrong for counsel to appear for the prosecution in a criminal case if he knew that a deliberate attempt was being made to convict an innocent man. Different considerations arise when appearing on behalf of a prisoner: here the defence has the right to have the charge proved beyond reasonable doubt. If the prisoner has admitted his guilt to his counsel, the position is more difficult, because counsel cannot call the prisoner into the witness-box to give evidence that he is innocent: such a course would make counsel an accessory to the prisoner's perjury. The same objection would apply to calling witnesses to prove an alibi or any other positive defence which cannot be true, having regard to the prisoner's admitted guilt. If, in such circumstances, the confession is made before the trial, it is in general the duty of counsel to withdraw from the case, unless the prisoner is content, after the position has been explained to him, to put forward a negative defence.

In general, the rights and privileges exercised by an advocate are those which his client could exercise if appearing in person. The advocate must treat the court with respect, while at the same time insisting on freedom to present his case to the fullest extent necessary. He has no right, however, to make attacks against third parties unless these are connected with the issues in the case and are based on sufficient grounds. This matter generally arises in connection with cross-examination and will be explained in more detail in discussing that subject.

3 The branches of advocacy

The technique of advocacy falls naturally into three branches.

In the first place there is the technique involved in the speeches and the formulation of arguments. This is the art of *oratory*, or *rhetoric*, which has been studied since before the time of Aristotle, with the result that it is well understood.

In the second place it is necessary to know how to ask questions in examination-in-chief and cross-examination. This is the art of *interrogation*, and plainly there is a technique for this, though it has not been analysed so fully as the technique of speaking.

Finally, there is the question of strategy and tactics in the conduct of the entire case. There is little technique in this, because it is mainly a matter of practical judgment, but at the same time there are some useful lines of approach which can be suggested.

The following chapters deal with each of these subjects in turn. The examination of witnesses, which is the most difficult accomplishment of all, has been set in the forefront and is illustrated by numerous examples from reported trials.

Chapter 2

The General Technique of Interrogation and the Fallacies of Testimony

1 Methods of interrogation

Before we turn to the technique of examination-in-chief and cross-examination in open court, it will be useful to analyse the methods of interrogating witnesses from a more general point of view. What is the technique followed by an impartial investigator — such as a detective officer — whose object is to ensure that the whole truth is discovered?[3]

The first approach, no doubt, will be to ask the witness to relate his story in his own words: 'Please tell me everything you know about this affair.' Let us suppose, to take a concrete example, that a murder is being investigated, and that the witness spent the evening with the victim and was the last person to see him. The investigator will probably say: 'Describe what happened during the evening

---

[3] See generally H. Gross *Criminal Investigation* (4th ed., 1949) Chap. II, pp. 27-60, and Soderman & O'Connell, *Modern Criminal Investigation* (1938), pp. 5-33, both of which have provided some of the material for this chapter.

until the deceased left you.' After the statement has been taken down, various methods may be used, according to the circumstances, to make sure that it is complete and reliable. It may be necessary to ask the witness to fill in more details to amplify his statement and to explain ambiguities. At this stage the witness must of course be guided in the right direction, but he must not be asked *suggestive* questions, that is to say questions which suggest what the answer be. Thus he should not be asked: 'Was X — wearing a green hat?' but 'Was X — wearing anything on his head?' and if the answer is 'Yes', then 'What was it?' The importance of avoiding suggestive questions at the outset — as will appear shortly in connection with the fallacies of testimony — is that, if the witness's recollection is vague, his imagination will quickly get to work to fill in the gaps as soon as a definite picture is suggested to him.

It may be necessary to assist the memory of the witness. Here it is best to avoid a strained effort to recollect the missing details, and to take the witness back to the scene as it was at the time, or just before, so that he can revisualise the events as they happened, and be helped by the association of ideas.

The next stage will be to straighten out the chronology and get the evidence in the right order. At the same time it will be useful to obtain details of the general background — such things as the position of furniture in a room, or of rooms in a building, when relevant.

Prima facie, the witness has now given his complete story. However, some of his statements may seem open to doubt, or there may be reason to suspect that he is not telling the truth. Therefore, the investigator may go over the details thoroughly, and ask searching questions with the object of discovering inconsistencies, improbabilities, and unreliable factors on which the statement is based. For instance, the witness may have said that, after he left the deceased, he saw X — walking along the road in the same direction as the deceased: and he may be asked how he recognised X — , whether by his face, his figure, his walk or something else.

This may be described as *the technique of probing*.

After probing into the details as far as he wishes, the investigator, we may suppose, will go away, take statements from other witnesses, and examine the scene of the crime. As a result of these further inquiries, various facts may come to light which clash with the statements of the original witness. Let it be assumed, for example, that according to the fresh evidence, this witness did not leave the deceased at the stated time and place, but was afterwards seen walking back with the deceased in the direction of his house, where the murder took place. Let it be further assumed that the murder was committed with a paper knife, which is said to be the property of this witness, and that his fingerprints are identified on the knife. The investigator will of course return and use these facts, in his further investigation, to break down or modify the original story. This use of awkward facts against a witness may be called the *the technique of confrontation* or *firm insinuation*.

A skilful questioner, in using this technique to destroy part of a witness's statement and so to discover the real truth of the matter, will be particularly careful not to use all his material at once, for in doing so he may be met with a plausible explanation which is consistent with all of it. Instead, he will start by pinning down the witness to exact and unmistakable statements on that part of his story which is suspected, in order to prevent him from wriggling out of it in the face of the fresh evidence. Afterwards, he will introduce the damaging facts one by one, reserving the worst till the last.

We shall come back to this method again in dealing with cross-examination, but the subject is so important that it is worth while to develop the imaginary case a little further.

The investigator, then, might start quite innocently on the following lines:

> 'When I saw you before, you told me that you left the deceased just before half-past nine, outside the restaurant where you had dinner together. Is that right ?' - 'Yes'
>
> 'Are you certain about the time?' - 'Yes, I looked at my watch as I left him.'
>
> 'And you didn't walk home with him that night?' - 'No.'
>
> 'Did you walk in the same direction as the deceased for a short distance?' - 'No, I went the other way.'
>
> 'Do you know Mr. Brown?' - 'Oh yes, I know him quite well.'
>
> 'Is he a reliable man?' - 'Yes.'
>
> 'Do you know that Mr. Brown saw you walking with the deceased at ten o'clock, half an hour after you say you had left him?'

This introduces the first damaging fact. When the witness has tied himself up in explaining this, the question of the paper-knife may be introduced, first in an innocent way, asking the witness whether he owns such a knife, then confronting him with its discovery at the scene of the crime. If the explanation offered is that it has been missing for some time and must have been stolen, the witness will be faced with the third and most damaging fact — the fingerprints.

This is, of course, an extreme case, as the witness may be the actual murderer: but extreme cases are sometimes effective illustrations.

There are many cases, however, where no question of confrontation can arise, and the witness seems to be perfectly truthful. Yet the investigator may feel that the evidence is all pointing in one direction, and that possibly the witness has placed a one-sided interpretation on the facts. To test this he may suggest other possible interpretations, possible explanatory facts which might give the evidence a new turn. This is *the technique of gentle insinuation*.

Lastly, having exhausted the subject of the original

enquiry — the evening of the murder, in the example quoted — the investigator may strike out on a new line altogether, for instance by asking the witness if he knows anything about the financial affairs of the murdered man.

The three techniques of confrontation or firm insinuation, probing and insinuation are the foundation of cross-examination, and in Chapter 5 we shall return to them in great detail. Alternatively, we may say there are two techniques only: probing, and insinuation in both its forms.

In conclusion, there is one principle which is paramount in all forms of interrogation, viz. that it is necessary to frame questions which are as simple and clear as possible. This ensures that there is no mistake or waste of time in understanding the question: it also ensures that there is no mistake about what is admitted or denied in answering it.

The application of the techniques which have been outlined above will vary according to the witness. Witnesses may be divided into two broad classes: those who honestly wish to speak the truth (but are quite likely to be mistaken) and those who do not. The following sections of this chapter deal with these two classes in turn.

2 Mistakes made by a truthful witness: the fallacies of testimony[4]

The most honest witnesses frequently give evidence which is unsound, though they are quite sure that it is true.

Indeed, it has been estimated by psychologists and by experienced judges that something like one-fourth of the evidence given by truthful witnesses is unreliable.

[4]   This section is based in part on Prof. E. J. Swift, *Psychology and the Day's Work,* Chap. VIII, the Psychology of Testimony and Rumour, pp. 273-313: see also Francis L. Wellman, *The Art of Cross-examination* (1928) Chap. VIII and Prof. Hugo Munsterberg, *On the Witness Stand.*

Such mistakes arise from several sources. They may, for instance, be due to:

(i)   Errors of the senses, that is to say faulty observation in the first place;

(ii)   Errors of interpretation;

(iii)   Errors of the memory and the imagination — two faculties which interact closely with one another;

(iv)   Errors of expression, especially in the form of exaggeration.

It is usual to add, as further sources of error, the influence of the emotions, and of bias or partisanship. These, however, are not direct sources of error: they are remoter causes, in that they may cause faulty observation, or set the imagination to work, or lead to exaggeration in giving evidence. The exposure of honest mistakes plays a great part in cross-examination, and therefore it is essential to examine each of the sources of error in turn and to show how mistakes can arise.

(i) Faulty observation: errors of the senses

Leaving aside documentary proof, all evidence given in the courts is founded, directly or ultimately, on the evidence of the senses, that is to say on things seen, heard, smelt, tasted or felt — but pre-eminently on things seen or heard. The following remarks relate to observation in its general meaning, not merely to things seen but also to perception by the other senses: and some illustrations are given of possible lines of cross-examination, though these belong more properly to a later chapter.

Accurate observation depends on many factors, but the most fundamental is the *opportunity* to observe — being in the right position and at the right distance, for example, and the state of visibility or the amount of noise going on. If it can be shown that there was no proper opportunity to see or hear what was going on, the evidence can be undermined or at all events greatly shaken. There is a good illustration in the trial of Dickman.[5] The prisoner was charged with murdering a man who was travelling in a railway carriage to pay wages at a colliery. Identification rested, in part, on the statement of the murdered man's wife, who stood at the door of the carriage for a few seconds and saw a man, sitting there with her husband, whom she identified as the prisoner. Mitchell-Innes, K.C., cross-examined as follows:

    'The shadow was right on to the man?' — 'Right on to him'

    'He had his hat on?' — 'Yes'

    'His collar held up in the way you have described?' — 'Held up.'

This was not, of course, conclusive, but went a long way to weaken the widow's evidence, if it had stood alone.

Opportunity to observe is not in itself enough. There is a familiar experiment in which a picture is shown to several people, and after they have looked at it for a few moments they are asked to write down the details. Most people are unable to write down very much. Exceptionally, a trained observer, such as a police officer, may notice every detail of a scene. As a rule, the ordinary man does not notice much unless his attention is attracted and his interest aroused. *Interest and attention* are pre-conditions of accurate observation. Every day, numerous things are said and done in our presence which we hardly notice. It follows that evidence given by a witness about matters in which he took no interest at the time is likely to be vague: positive statements by such a witness are likely to be unreliable, as they may have been built up after the event by inference and imagination. Thus in the ordinary road accident case, a bystander is unlikely to see much until his attention is attracted by a loud crash. Likewise, where a third party reports a casual conversation which he heard some months before, and which has become important only because a

---

[5]   *The Trial of Dickman,* ed. by S. O. Rowan-Hamilton (1914), p. 58. This is an unusually instructive case.

dispute has afterwards arisen, it is improbable that he noticed or remembered the exact words which were used.

There are other limitations to accuracy: if events happen quickly, or there is a great deal of talk going on within a short space of time, an impartial witness will see or hear only a fraction of what is happening.[6] Surprise, excitement and rush make the picture confused and its details obscure. If the witness has a personal interest or bias, his attention will tend to be concentrated on facts or remarks which are favourable to him, to the exclusion of others. Prof. Swift says (*op. cit.*, p. 307):

> 'Attention is rigorously selective, and this selection is based on the relative importance of the details; but it should be remembered that the choice of what is important is a personal matter.'

He is referring, of course, not to a deliberate choice, but to one which takes place subconsciously. It is well to realise that bias can intervene, without any dishonest intent, even at the stage of observation, before memory and imagination have got to work.

Pausing here, it is evident that there is great scope for the technique of *probing* in testing the accuracy of observation. One familiar device, where a witness claims to have seen certain details, is to lead him to say something more, which can be disproved. In one case a police witness gave evidence identifying a man, and Sir Henry Curtis-Bennett, K.C., led him on to deny that the man had a limp: the limp, however, was proved to be real. A similar device can be used where a witness swears that certain words were never used: he is led on to say he never heard certain other words, and it is proved that those other words were in fact spoken.

A further factor which may interfere with accuracy is the

[6] See, for instance, the conflicting evidence in *The Laski Libel Action* (Daily Express, 1947), which concerned remarks made in the excitement of a political meeting.

presence of intense pain, or shock, or strong emotion: all these things may prevent the senses from operating in a natural way, and may produce pictures or sounds which are distorted, or totally imaginary. Hallucinations, which are an extreme example, may originate from drugs, or drink, or from illnesses affecting the brain. A person who is seriously ill may easily hear imaginary voices, and be quite convinced that they are real. The reason is that, in abnormal physical states, there is less interest in exterior happenings and the imagination takes the place of the exterior senses. Strong emotion may have the same effect as shock or pain, though the effect is not so obvious. Any condition which concentrates attention on one's own interior feelings — mental or physical — is open to suspicion, because it draws attention away from the outside world and gives scope to the imagination.

The negative side of these conclusions ought not to be exaggerated. The positive side is this: that if a witness is, to a reasonable extent, impartial, and interested in what is going on around him, and is in a normal state of health, his evidence will be reliable in substance though not in every detail. Cross-examination of such a witness will mainly be directed to weakening statements of too positive a character, and to suggesting other possibilities and explanatory facts: in short, the main technique used will be *insinuation,* assisted and introduced by a little *probing.* As for biased witnesses, at least they do not fail to notice facts which tell in their own favour, and, as the witnesses on the other side will be equally positive on the facts which tell in their favour, the technique of *confrontation* can often be brought into play.

We now turn to particular forms of sense-observation.

(a) *Seeing.* The eyes are seldom fixed on the same object for a long period of time. For example, a bystander who is watching traffic just before a collision will see motor-cars in different positions at different times, but is not likely to be watching one of them continuously: or if he is watching one, he will miss the others. The successive pictures are linked together by imagination and inference. (Here it may be remarked that the imagination is not necessarily building up false pictures, but playing a perfectly natural role in constructing a consistent picture from a variety of sense data: it does not, *ipso facto*, introduce error, but only the possibility of error.) The corollary is that an eye-witness may miss quite an important incident — for instance, the actual angle of collision — if his eye has strayed away at that point of time: this happens much more easily when events follow one another quickly.

Another characteristic of visual observation is its vagueness, for instance, in noticing the colour of clothing, or shapes, or faces. Indeed, vagueness is a sign of truth, while evidence of a positive kind is unreliable, unless the witness is a keen observer. Here is an illustration, quoted at random from the trial of Mrs. Duncan.[7] John Maude, K.C. (for the prosecution) is cross-examining a witness who saw a 'spirit-form' at a spiritualist seance, the object of the prosecution being to show that the 'spirit-form' was faked by the medium with the help of a white cloth.

'Have you seen Albert?' — 'In spirit form, yes.'

'Albert, as we have heard of him?' — 'Yes.'

'What did he look like?' — 'He is a very tall gentleman and I should think he was dark and he had a beard.'

'Could you see his hair?' — 'I cannot say that, but he had a beard.'

'Could you see his hair or not?' — 'I can't remember.'

'What else did you see?' — 'I saw him, that is all.'

'Describe what you saw of him.' — 'A very tall gentleman.'

'What about his face?' — 'I think it was a longish face.'

'Can you tell us anything more about it? Had he got a moustache or beard?' — 'I said a beard.'

---

7   *The Trial of Mrs. Duncan,* ed. by C. E. Bechhofer Roberts. (1945) at p. 157.

'A long beard or a short beard?' — 'Not too long.'

'About how long?' — 'I am a poor judge: I cannot say feet.'

'No, not feet, that would be phenomenal. Was it a three inch beard or just a little hair round the face? . . .' — 'I will answer if the lady and gentlemen will not laugh . . .'

'All I am asking you is this. Could you really see a beard that projects from the face?' — 'Yes.'

'Or could you simply see as you thought hair round the face, close to it?' — 'Here.'

'Is it here — just close to the face?' — 'Well, I can say beard, that is all I can say.'

In this instance, of course, the light was very dim when the 'spirit-form' was seen: nevertheless the vagueness of the evidence is typical of descriptions by witnesses of faces and shapes which have been seen for a short time.

The possibility of optical illusion ought to be kept in mind. Frequently, when photographs are produced, the witness is asked whether the slopes have not been fore-shortened, so as to look less steep than they really are.[8] Experienced mountaineers know that a hillside looks steep from above, but quite a gentle slope from below: the most accurate view is from the side, where the exact angle can be seen. Illusions are easily created by moonlight, and also by headlights on a dark road. There was a good example in the trial of Lord de Clifford for manslaughter, where Lord de Clifford saw headlights approaching round a bend, thought that they were on the wrong side of the road, and moved to his own wrong side to avoid a collision.[9]

(b) *Hearing.* Sometimes a case turns on inarticulate noises,

---

[8]   This point was of some consequence in *The Arran Murder* and in *The Trial of Ley and Smith* — both of which are quoted later.

[9]   See *'Curtis': The Life of Sir Henry Curtis-Bennett*, K.C., by Roland Wild and Derek Curtis-Bennett (1937), pp. 284 - 6.

such as the crash of a collision, or the sound of a shot or a scuffle.

More often, evidence of things heard consists of conversations. These may be conversations overheard at or before the commission of a crime, or, in civil litigation, conversations resulting in agreements which have not been committed to writing. In both cases, a slight difference of wording may be quite important.

Now the ears (like the eyes) do not as a rule give continuous attention to what is going on. A salient word stands out here and there, and the general drift of a conversation is followed rather than every word. A person who is interested in the result of the conversation will listen more keenly than a bystander: but everyone hears so much talk going on throughout the day that it would be exceedingly difficult to pay attention to most of it. Particular remarks will stand out only if they seemed at the time to be very striking or very interesting: otherwise, it is unlikely that a bystander will be able to quote *the actual words* unless he made a note at once.

But, as witnesses do claim to remember the exact words, it is evident that there is good scope for cross-examination. This will take the form of suggesting to the witness that what he heard was something slightly different in sound, but very different in effect. (This is an application of the technique of insinuation.) Two illuminating examples are quoted in the biography of Marshall Hall.[10] In the first case a woman was on trial for the murder of her illegitimate child, the defence being that the death was accidental. She was alleged to have asked, shortly before the death: 'How can anyone get rid of a baby?' Marshall Hall asked the witnesses whether she did not really say: 'How *can* anyone get rid of a baby like this!' — as if she meant that she would never dream of getting rid of it. The witnesses agreed with his suggestion, and, by the slight change of emphasis,

[10]   Marjoribanks, *op. cit.,* pp 127-9, 399-401.

the phrase took on an opposite meaning. In the other case, Ronald Light was charged with the murder of a girl named Bella. He was the last person to be seen with her, and the possibility of a motive depended largely on whether he had known the girl beforehand or had met her as a complete stranger, as he claimed. The girl's uncle had heard Light say to her:

'Bella, I thought you had gone the other way.'

The use of the name Bella (if proved) was an important point against the prisoner. Marshall Hall asked the uncle whether the words might not have been:

'Hello, I thought you had gone the other way.'

The uncle would not admit this, but the mere putting of the question showed the jury that he might be mistaken.

(c) *Taste, smell and touch.* These three senses may be grouped together, because they are all more subjective and relative, and therefore vaguer, than sight and hearing. Evidence of smell frequently appears in cases, but is usually indecisive, for example in the trial of Dr. Ruxton, who murdered his wife and cut up the body in the house. (There was evidence of some sort of smell from a locked room where the body had probably been dissected.) The following illustration, which indicates the vagueness of this sort of evidence, is again taken from the trial of Mrs. Duncan, where John Maude, K.C., cross-examining a defence witness, is trying to establish that there was an objectionable smell, which would support the prosecution theory that Mrs. Duncan was regurgitating muslin to simulate 'spirit-forms.'[11]

'Did you ever notice any curious smell at these seances?' — 'Yes, sir, the ectoplasm does smell rather faint,'

'Rather what?' — 'Faint.'

'What sort of smell?' — 'Not a bad smell.'

'Do you know what a corpse smells like?' — 'It would be

[11]   *Op. cit.*, p. 174.

something like that.'

'Did it smell anything like vomit?' — 'No, nothing objectionable.'

'Is that the nearest thing you can think of?' — 'You have mentioned a corpse.'

'Was it like any known scent?' — 'No.'

'Was it sweet?' — 'No, I would not call it sweet, but it was not objectionable.'

(ii) Faulty interpretation

Mere observation by means of the eyes and the other senses is only one stage in the process of gaining knowledge about things and events. Simultaneously, there is a complex integration of imagination, inference and previous experience by which the phenomena observed are *interpreted*. For instance, we see a moving patch of white, shaped in a certain way, accompanied by loud honking noise, and thereupon we say to ourselves: 'That is a swan.' The distinguished philosopher, Alfred North Whitehead, makes the following comment:[12]

'Direct visual observation is concerned with the vision of coloured shapes in motion — "questionable shapes". Direct aural observation is concerned with auditions of sounds. But some contemporary observer of such shapes and noises, for example, some envoy resident at a foreign Court, interpreting the so-called "bare" facts, states that "he interviewed the minister of state, who manifested considerable emotion and explained with great clearness the measures with which he would meet the impending crisis". In such ways contemporary evidence is contemporary interpretation, including the assumption of data other than these bare sensa.'

Errors can easily creep into this process of interpretation — theories or facts wrongly assumed, mistaken inferences or mistaken analogies. The trial of Mrs. Duncan, already quoted, is an excellent example. The defence witnesses

[12] *Adventures of Ideas* (1933), pp. 3-4.

accepted spiritualistic theories concerning the materialisation of 'spirit-forms' and 'ectoplasm', and everything they saw and heard was interpreted on this basis. The cross-examination was a prolonged application of the technique of probing, to disclose the flaws of reasoning, in combination with the use of insinuation, to suggest another interpretation — that Mrs. Duncan was impersonating the 'spirits' with the aid of a dark background, a dim light and a drapery of butter muslin (which the witness called 'a spirit robe').

An outstanding example of interpreting sense data is *identification*. Identification is, taken generally, the most shaky of all forms of evidence. It may take two forms, of which a specimen of the first would be:

'I saw a man, whom I recognised as X.'

An accurate identification in this form depends on several links, each of which may be open to attack:

1. 'I knew X quite well beforehand, and had seen him several times.'
2. 'I had a clear view of the man on this occasion.'
3. 'I recognised him because of his eyes, nose and moustache' (or by his voice, or method of walking, or perhaps just by a general impression).

The other form of identification (more common in criminal cases) would be this:

'I saw a man (committing burglary, or as the case may be). The prisoner is the man I saw.'

This also depends on several links; e.g.

1. 'I had a clear view of the man'
2. 'I noticed his face and his voice.'
3. 'I recognised the prisoner's face at the identification parade, and I also recognise his voice.'

An attack on identification will therefore take the form of a searching inquiry into the detailed grounds on which identification is based.

There are a number of other cases, frequently encountered in the courts, where evidence is given which appears at first sight to be a simple statement of fact, but is really the result of a complex process of interpretation. Here are some illustrations:

A bystander in a traffic accident:
'The car was travelling at 40 miles an hour.'

A policeman:
'I saw at once that the accused was drunk.'

A doctor:
'I conducted the post-mortem examination. Death was due to heart attack.'

A land agent:
'I have seen the plaintiff's farm. It was in first-class condition and worth £10,000.'

In all these cases the technique of probing can be used, first of all to unravel complex facts into their separate elements, as in mathematics a vector of force is resolved into component forces acting at right angles, and secondly to test the validity, one by one, of the component facts relied on. Further, in interpretation as in perception, bias or emotion may exercise a dominant influence.

So far, we are concerned only with eye-witnesses. Similar remarks apply to the questioning of experts on opinion evidence, but there are also other factors, and this subject is referred to later.

(iii) Errors of the memory and imagination

The memory and imagination are often separated when the fallacies arising from them are explained, but mistakes really arise because the two act in conjunction. At the moment experiences are recalled for the first time memory (of the contemporary *interpretation,* of course) is probably quite accurate, but if the picture is at all dim the imagination steps in, quite normally and naturally, to complete the details.

The only real fault with memory itself is that it becomes more and more vague with the lapse of time. The original observation, as already explained, may have been vague to start with. If the witness was interested and attentive, the observation will be more clear-cut and the memory more exact. Prof. Swift says: 'Interest and attention, to be sure, tend to fix facts and descriptions in memory.' Yet even a clear impression may be obscured after a long time.

Vagueness in recollection, whether there was vagueness at the start or not, is the greatest of all sources of error. To quote Prof. Swift again:

> 'The undetected vagueness of memory-details of the witnesses furnishes a fertile soil for the growth of imaginary pictures. The attempt to see faces in the moon is comparable to their experience. With a dim outline, or a sketch with several possibilities, there is always a strong tendency to fill in the outlines, usually with what is in one's mind.'[13]

Attention may now be drawn to several factors which *accentuate* this natural tendency for the imagination to supplement the memory.

The first of these factors is a sudden happening, *just after* the events in question, which rivets the attention of the observer, previously roving at large and in a superficial manner. Such a happening is the crash of a motor-car collision, or a sudden quarrel. On these occasions, the mind of the observer flashes back at once to the preceding events and commences to reconstruct them. Afterwards, the vague impression received at the time will be blended with the reconstruction, and both will be remembered together as a single vivid picture seen at the time.

Apart from such dramatic incidents, as soon as any happenings become a matter of controversy the witnesses are liable to talk them over and think about them. Each time the picture may be filled out a little, or something may be omitted, and when it is again recalled the memory has again been modified.

A third factor, especially in murder cases, may be Press

[13]   *Op. cit.*, p. 287, p. 277.

publicity or local rumour, which the witnesses unconsciously absorb and which forms a prejudicial background to their evidence. A somewhat similar result may be produced if one witness reads the statement of another:[14] anything which puts a vivid picture before the witness is liable to influence his imagination.

Finally, there is the effect of suggestive questions — and it is for this reason that an impartial investigator is careful to avoid suggestive questions in the early stages of his inquiries: the technique of insinuation, which is inherently suggestive, is brought to bear only when the evidence has crystallised in a one-sided form, as is the case at the stage of cross-examination. Prof. Swift[15] quotes an impressive illustration of the effect of suggestion, in a murder case which occurred in the American Middle West and was investigated thirty years afterwards. Among other things it was alleged that the body had been taken away in a covered wagon, hidden under a buffalo robe. He says:

'The detectives, as they secured one fact after another, collected the information by suggestive questions and statements to those with whom they conversed. When, for example, a prospective witness said that there was a buffalo robe in the wagon the detectives would ask if it covered the outlines of a human form. The man would think it likely, and soon that it did . . . It is a well-known principle of psychology that if you tell a man something often enough he finally accepts it; and as he continually repeats it, even as a possible fact, it ends by becoming firmly fixed. Then he believes he saw or heard it.'

Throughout all this ferment of memory and imagination, the emotions, or bias, or wishful thinking, exercise a pervading influence, both in suppressing real facts and in causing the acceptance of fresh details which are imagined.

---

[14] For an interesting cross-examination on this point, too long and inconclusive to reproduce here, see *The Trial of Merrett* ed by W. Roughead (1929) at pp. 123-5.
[15] *Op. cit.*, pp. 276, 277.

Prof. Swift sums up the whole subject as follows:[16]

> '. . . memory is exceedingly plastic and prone to error; and
> it is always exposed to the deflecting influences of repeated
> narration, with its generous mixture of error, continuous
> thinking about the affair with numerous fictitious
> insertions, intended actions not carried out, biased
> opinions, and suggestions.'

It is a difficult task to detect and expose errors which have
arisen from these causes: the only method is to apply the
technique of probing at every weak point, and, so far as this
is successful, to insinuate the version which is believed to
be correct. Confrontation may also be employed, if strong
material is available.

(iv) Errors of expression

A witness may know exactly what he wishes to say, but
fail to express himself correctly. This does not call for
much detailed comment, though it sometimes gives scope
for a pointed cross-examination.

First in degree of importance are exaggerations. A
witness may say that he saw X — at a certain place and
time, and may then be asked:

> 'Did you know X — ?' — 'Oh yes, I have seen him many
> times before.'

On being further pressed, he may be forced to admit that
he has only seen him twice.

Sometimes a witness answers a question which he does
not understand. Lord Justice Wrottesley quotes[17] a case
where a Scottish ghillie showed the size of a fish and was
then asked whether this was the the 'average' size of the
fish taken in the loch, to which the old man replied 'Yes'.
The following cross-examination ensued:

> 'And what d'ye understand by the word "aver-r-rage"?'
> 'Ah've no idea.'

---

[16]   *Op, cit.,* p. 287.
[17]   *Letters to a Young Barrister,* p. 57.

Every day, witnesses make casual slips in terminology: a witness may talk about the offside of his car when he means the nearside, and a non-nautical witness may get mixed up between starboard and port. Those of us who have served in the forces can well remember the recruit who turns left upon the order 'Right — turn!' Care must be taken during examination-in-chief to correct such slips, which may give rise to great confusion.

3 Witnesses who do not wish to tell the truth

This class of witnesses, we may suppose, know the truth perfectly well, but do not wish to reveal it. The complex psychological questions connected with faulty observation, interpretation and memory do not arise. At the stage of expression, the witness knows the true facts, but withholds them. His motive is usually strong bias or self-interest: the presence of these factors, the more so if reinforced by indications of a dishonest character, will suggest to the interrogator that he may be dealing with a witness who is not truthful.

There are two cases. One of these, of course, is the deliberate liar. The other is the witness who, while taking great care to speak the literal truth, is yet keeping something back. The tactics to be employed against a witness of the latter kind are first, the technique of probing, to search for the weak point; secondly, the technique of insinuation, to put positively to the witness the part of the story which he is believed to be hiding.[18]

---

[18] Sir Henry Hawkins, Q.C. (later Lord Brampton) had a wonderful flair for detecting the weak point in such cases — an example of *practical judgment,* referred to at pp. 5-6, ante. For an illustrations see his Reminiscences (1906), pp. 90-95. *Stone* (op. cit. p. 2 note 1, *supra*) has useful guidelines on deciding whether a witness is lying.

The interrogation of a witness who is deliberately lying is a more complex matter. To enter into a lengthy discussion at this stage would anticipate the chapters on cross-examination, and therefore only a few general indications are offered, which may serve as an introduction to the subject.

Lying witnesses do not form a single class. They range through all types, from the childish amateur to the accomplished storyteller. Most readers will recall the facts of the Tichborne case, where a butcher's boy arrived from Australia and masqueraded as the missing heir to the Tichborne estates, who had vanished years before in South America. An important question was whether the missing heir had tattoo marks on his arms. Bogle, his negro servant, who had rallied to the support of the claimant, deposed that there were no such marks. Sir Henry Hawkins cross-examined the witness as to the circumstances in which he had seen Richard Tichborne's arms, and elicited the absurd story that he had twice seen his master roll up his sleeves to scratch for a flea. That is an example of a *foolish* liar. Another example is to be found in *The Trial of Ley and Smith*,[19] where Ley was charged with tying up a man in his house and murdering him: here a defence witness came forward with the lame story that he had wandered into the house, found a man tied to a chair, and pulled accidentally on the ropes — the inference being — in exoneration of Ley — that the intruder had killed the man by misadventure. Under cross-examination the story appeared quite ridiculous.

These illustrations are quoted to show that it is not always difficult to expose a false story. On the other hand, it is very hard to break down a man who tells a consistent, well-thought-out story. However, there are two powerful factors which work in favour of the interrogator. The first is

[19]   Ed. F. T. Jesse (1947), pp. 208-222. The whole passage is most amusing and well worth reading at length.

that it requires great inventive power to keep up a false story, especially if it has to be enlarged in all sorts of new directions. Furthermore, every time the story is amplified, there is an increased risk that it will come into conflict with indisputable facts. In the second place, it is usually impossible to tell a story which is not a mixture of truth and falsehood: and if, exceptionally, false evidence is complete and self-contained (as in the case of a faked alibi), it still has to fit in with surrounding circumstances; the fringes of the story, in time and place, must have a point of junction with the world of fact and reality. It follows that it ought to be possible to draw out contradictions from the evidence; and, given plenty of time, a police investigator generally feels confident that he can demolish a false story. If it is not so easy for a cross-examiner, the reason is that he does not have unlimited time at his disposal. The judge may become impatient at a lengthy cross-examination if no results are in sight.

The most powerful weapon which can be used to destroy false evidence is the technique of massive confrontation, which is firm confrontation in its strongest form. This technique, at its best, may be compared to a creeping artillery barrage, driving back the enemy foot by foot. For this purpose it is essential to have ammunition, consisting of damaging facts and documents which cannot be denied. The ammunition should not be fired all at once, but by degrees. Confrontation, properly used, involves first of all presenting an adverse fact and then tying down the witness to detailed explanations: then presenting further facts, and exacting further explanations, until eventually the witness is led into contradictions.

Failing material for this, the technique of probing may be used in rather a special way, by leading the witness to enlarge on his story until he gives details which can be contradicted. Thus, in testing a false alibi concerning a particular evening, the events of that evening can be linked up with the earlier part of the day, or with other days in the same week, and this may result in displacing the date or the time deposed to.

There are other possible lines of attack, using the method of insinuation. Starting from admitted facts, the cross-examiner may move quite gently and cautiously towards damaging admissions, taking care to conceal from the witness the object of his questions. Alternatively, if the story is partly true and partly false, he may base his attack on the true part of the story and drive home, one by one, all the adverse inferences which can be drawn from it. This is *firm insinuation* in a less massive form, using at least some incontrovertible facts, as opposed to *gentle insinuation*. There is a fine example in the trial of Crippen for poisoning his wife, where the prisoner could not conceal that he had fled from the country in disguise, and Sir Richard Muir, K.C., drove home all the implications of guilt which followed from this (see p.96 *post*).

It is best, of course, to show the inherent falsity of a story by cross-examining on the facts. There is, however, yet another method, by questioning the witness on collateral matters which affect his credit. The object here is to undermine the evidence by establishing that he cannot be believed: and this method may be called, for greater vividness, *the technique of undermining*.

All these techniques are analysed and reviewed at length in Chapter 5.

Chapter 3

Examination-in-Chief

1. The general background

Its central role

One sometimes hears discussions on the relative importance of examination-in-chief, cross-examination and the speeches. These discussions are really unprofitable, because the relative importance varies from case to case. However, it is at least clear that examination-in-chief plays a central role. No civil claim, and no prosecution, can succeed unless it is sustained by the evidence. It is the role of examination-in-chief to present this evidence in a complete and convincing form, and the evidence-in-chief is therefore the pivot of the whole case. Sometimes, especially in the county courts and the justices' courts, there are no speeches; sometimes, too, there is no cross-examination; but no ordinary case can conducted without evidence-in-chief. Exceptionally, the defence may submit that there is no case to answer, in which event success depends on the speech making the submission. In the higher courts, also, where points of law are argued, the speeches stand alone. For the average advocate, however, these exceptional cases are only a small percentage of his practice.

It follows from these remarks that the first branch of his

art which an advocate must learn is examination-in-chief.

The proofs

If, ordinarily speaking, the case centres on the evidence-in-chief, this in turn is founded on the statements of witnesses, or proofs (precognitions, as they are called in Scotland). A few words on the taking of the proofs will therefore not be out of place.

Statements ought to be taken from the witnesses at the earliest opportunity. The details fade with the lapse of time, and the evidence becomes modified under the influence of imagination.[20] The taking of proofs is often delayed in a civil action because it is thought that there will be a settlement. This is a serious error. Apart from the blurring of memory, there is always the possibility that the witnesses will be interviewed by the other side, and the further risk that, by reason of insufficient knowledge, the claim may be based on mistaken grounds. Reports from medical and technical experts are another matter: it may be convenient to defer these, on grounds of expense, until it is clear that the claim will be contested, though even here there should be no delay if the judgment of the expert depends on seeing the evidence while it is fresh. Also, in civil cases (e.g. medical negligence), it is often impossible to formulate the claim without expert advice.

In taking a proof, it is best in the first place to ask the witness to tell his story, just noting the salient facts and dates. When the outline is clear, the statement should be taken down in chronological order, amplifying the details at the same time: doubtful points should be tested at once by a few searching questions.

The ideal proof contains all the facts in the right order. It also contains complete details, some of which counsel may not wish to bring out, but they should be there so that he can use his discretion. The ideal proof contains, besides,

[20]   See pp. 29-32 *ante*.

explanations in simple language of anything which might be obscure to the average man, such as the lay-out of a street or a house, or the working of a machine, or technical terms used in particular trades. Such explanations ought not to be left to the end, as footnotes so to speak, but ought to be introduced side by side with the part of the evidence which they are intended to clarify. Each stage in the evidence should be rounded off and completed before going on to the next.

Rules of law

The rules governing examination-in-chief are part of the law of evidence, and here attention is simply drawn to the outstanding points of practical importance. Evidence-in-chief is confined to relevant facts, i.e. those lawfully admissible in evidence, and hearsay is in general excluded. *Leading questions* must not be asked. These are not quite the same thing as suggestive questions. A suggestive question is one which conveys a vivid picture, and, if asked at the investigation stage, is liable to set the imagination of the witness to work and modify his evidence. A leading question is one which tells the witness what answer he is expected to give, and it is disallowed as a general rule because it would give an advocate an undue advantage in questioning his own witnesses. Leading questions are allowed, however, in two cases: (i) where the facts are not disputed, especially in introducing matter such as the name and address of the witness and his connection with the subject-matter of the case; and (ii) where it is necessary to obtain an express denial of some allegation.[21]

The aim of examination-in-chief

The aim of examination-in-chief is to elicit from the

[21] In theory, a leading question may also be asked to obtain a positive identification, but in practice it is usually better not to lead.

witness a complete, orderly story, told by the witness in his own natural way, with the minimum of prompting. The story should be in the right order, usually the order of time: if there are several distinct topics, they should be introduced one by one, according to their importance, each topic being exhausted before turning to the next. The story should be complete in detail, so far as is necessary for the proof of the case or to carry conviction, but this does not mean that it is necessary to go into minute details which have no substantial relevance: selection may be necessary.

2 The technique

The foundations

The foundations of technique in examination-in-chief are twofold. The first requisite is a firm grasp of the main lines of the evidence (and its place in the unfolding of the case). The ideal advocate does not examine from his proof — though he uses it to refresh his memory on dates and other details — but has absorbed the essentials of the story, so that the evidence is 'alive' for him and comes out effortlessly. The second requisite is skill in the use of words, so as to be able to guide the witness in the right direction without leading him. The choice of simple words is helpful: on the one hand a thing is always clearer if it is expressed simply, and on the other hand a relatively uneducated witness will have less difficulty in understanding what is said. One often hears pedantic questions such as this: 'Subsequent to that occurrence, what course of action did you take?' Why not say: 'What did you do after that?' Apart from using simple words, the questions themselves should be short and simple, as an intricate and complicated question is liable to confuse the witness, and thereupon there is a great waste of time in clearing up the confusion and splitting up the question into its component parts. Here, for instance, is a specimen of what ought not to be done, in a question put (in cross-examination) to the Tichborne claimant:

> 'When you say mathematics, what do you mean by mathematics? What are mathematics about? What did you learn? I will not ask you how far you went, but what sort of things did you learn in mathematics?'

An intelligent witness might be expected to say: 'One question at a time, please.'

Verbosity and ponderousness are cardinal faults in all forms of examination.

Guiding without leading

It has been said that the essence of successful examination-in-chief is 'to lead, without appearing to lead'. This is badly expressed, as it suggests a deliberate and cunning evasion of the rules of evidence. The true technique is to *guide* the witness without leading him. He must not be shown what answer is expected from him, but he ought to be given the clearest possible indication of the point on which his evidence is required, one way or the other. Thus it is wrong to ask: 'Was X — wearing a brown trilby hat?' The correct sequence is: 'Did X — have anything on his head?' 'What was it?' 'What sort of a hat?' 'What colour was it?' Again, it is wrong to ask: 'Did you see another car, coming very fast from the opposite direction?' The right sort of questions would be: 'Did you notice any other traffic?' 'Which direction was it coming from?' 'What speed was it travelling at?'

The last question might be framed in an alternative way, e.g. 'Was it going fast or slow?' These are obvious alternatives, one or other of them must be true, and there is nothing in the wording of the question to show which answer is desired. This method of framing questions in an alternative form can be extremely useful, but should not be abused, as would be the case if it introduced new and suggestive details which the witness might not have remembered on his own. For instance, the question about the hat might be framed in this way: 'Was X — wearing a brown trilby hat, or not?'; but it would still be a leading question. (If the evidence desired is simply whether a thing was so or not, the 'alternative' form of question is correct: but if the witness is being asked to give a description or reveal something new, the alternative form is wrong.)

Retaining control

Throughout the evidence-in-chief, the examiner must be in control, able to deflect the story in the right direction and away from irrelevancies: he must also be ready to check a loquacious witness, and to encourage one who is timid or hesitant. Occasionally it is convenient to say: 'Tell us about it in your own words.' Such a question should be limited to a particular phase of the evidence, e.g. 'Tell us in your own words what you saw at the moment of collision'. If the witness is allowed to give the whole of his evidence in his own way, he may miss out important points and stray into irrelevant details. In such a case the examiner is abdicating his function, and the judge may intervene and take the witness out of his hands.[22] If, of course, a witness is telling his story perfectly correctly and completely in his own way (as experts are often able to do), then he ought not to be interrupted, but the advocate must be ready to intervene if necessary.

The right order

If the court is to follow the evidence and understand it, the story must be told in the right order, which, in general, is the order of time. Each incident should be finished with before going on to the next. In a motor-accident case the order might be:

[22]   Thus in the *Trial of the Seddons* Bucknill J. said to the A.-G. 'Keep your witness in hand, Mr. Attorney.'

1. How the witness came to be on the scene;
2. What he saw of the movements of traffic before the accident;
3. What he saw at the moment of the accident; and
4. What he saw and heard afterwards.

If phases (2) and (3) are mixed up, the result will be confusion.

Some subjects do not lend themselves to this approach, and should therefore be dealt with in the order which is most natural. Thus an expert engineer, describing a machine which has caused an accident, should first be asked to explain the general nature and lay-out of this machine; then, the interconnection of the main parts; lastly, the detailed mechanism at the critical point where the accident occurred.

If there are several distinct topics, then they should be investigated in turn, and taken in the order which presents the case most easily to the mind of the court.

Thoroughness

Orderliness and thoroughness rank together as the leading principles of examination-in-chief. Every material detail must be brought out before moving on to the next stage. This does not mean that it is necessary to cover every detail set out in the proof: some of these may be irrelevant, as a proof should always contain too much rather than too little.[23] It is important, however, to avoid jumping from one subject to another in a disconnected manner, or going back in the story to bring out something which was carelessly overlooked. A consequence of these remarks is that examination-in-chief ought not to be hurried.

Among the material details which must be brought out at the time are explanations of points which are not readily

---

[23]   Similarly the prosecuting counsel in a criminal case is not bound to bring out the whole of the evidence in the depositions, but should use his judgment and bring out so much as is necessary or helpful.

understood, or which, though second nature to the witnesss, are obscure to the outsider. Such matters include the lay-out of rooms, or buildings, or streets, and the explanation of technical phrases or trade terminology.

Refreshing the memory of a witness

If a witness has difficulty in recalling a material fact, he should be guided to it as closely as possible without leading him. If he still cannot remember, he should not be pressed, because this may set up a mental strain which will make his memory more hazy than before. Instead, it is better to pass over the point for the time being, as if it did not greatly matter, and so allow the witness to relax. Afterwards, go back gently to the events leading up to the forgotten incident, and it is quite possible that the recollection will come back easily, stimulated, without strain, by the association of ideas.

As is well-known, a witness is allowed to refresh his own memory from a note made at the time of the occurrence, or shortly after it. This can be a great help in reporting conversations.

Toning down weak points

Where there is a weak point in the evidence, the manner of dealing with it may raise a difficult problem of practical judgment. It is the duty of counsel to treat the court with frankness, and certainly not to conceal facts if they are relevant: furthermore, if the point is brought out in cross-examination, its effect will be more damaging. As a rule, therefore, the better course is to bring out the point in examination-in-chief, without undue emphasis, and toning it down as far as the facts allow. Let us see how some leading advocates do it. Here, first of all, is Graham Murray (later Viscount Dunedin) examining for the prosecution in the Arran murder case,[24] where the body of a man had been found on a mountainside, and his companion was charged with murdering him. The defence were suggesting (among other things) that the place was dangerous and death might have been caused by an accidental fall.

> *Graham Murray.* — 'Was there anything in the character of the ground which would make it *specially* dangerous?' — 'No.'

Later in the same case, it appeared that the police, for some mysterious reason, had not kept the boots of the dead man, and the defence used this to raise vague suspicions. Graham Murray, examining a police witness, said to him:

> '*It seems* that you afterwards buried a pair of boots that were on the body?' — 'Yes, on the seashore at Corrie.'

The italics have been added in both illustrations to show how the question was toned down.

In *The Mr. A. Case,* [25] Sir John Simon, K.C., (later Viscount Simon) was in the awkward position of having to call a convicted man as the main witness for the defence. This is how he endeavoured to discount the fact:

> 'I am sorry to have to ask you, Mr. Newton, but I had better ask it here. Have you been convicted of forgery?' — 'Yes, I have, Sir John . . .'
> 'In the year 1907?' — 'I suppose that would be the year.'
> ' . . . and you served a sentence in respect of it?' — 'I did, yes.'

Notice the sympathetic atmosphere created, and the inference that, the sentence having been served, it was all over and done with.

---

24 *The Trial of John Watson Laurie,* ed. W. Roughead (1932), pp. 86, 88. This case is extremely interesting and it is also technically instructive. A reviewer of the 1st edition complained that I did not say whether he was convicted. He was.

25 Ed. C.E. Bechhofer Roberts, p. 261.

An illustration

Before closing this chapter, an illustration is given of a model examination-in-chief. This is taken from the Tichborne case,[26] where the defendants were seeking to show that there were tattoo marks on the arm of the false claimant. Notice the orderliness, the thoroughness at each stage, the precision with which the witness is guided to the exact point without leading (there are in fact a few leading questions), and the economy of words. The witness is Lord Bellew: the counsel is Henry Hawkins, Q.C. (later Lord Brampton), a most accomplished artist. The headings show the structure of the examination.

Introductory questions. First topic: knowledge of missing heir.

> 'I believe you were educated at Stonyhurst?' — 'I was.'
> 'Were you there with Roger Charles Tichborne?' —'Yes.'
> 'During what years were you with him?' — '1847 and 1848.'
> 'Were you both philosophers?' — 'Yes.'
> 'Where did you live?' — 'At a house called the seminary.'
> 'Did you both live in the seminary?' — 'We did.'
> 'During the years you were at Stonyhurst, did you see much of Roger Charles Tichborne?' — 'I did during the two years that we were together.'
> 'Were you in the same class?' — 'We were not in the same class exactly.'
> 'Where did you see most of him — At what parts of the day?' — 'During recreation.'
> 'Now, have you a recollection of the appearance of Roger Charles Tichborne?' — 'I have.'

Second topic: refusal to identify the claimant.

> 'You were in court, I think, during the time the claimant was under examination and cross-examination?' — 'I was

---

[26]   *The Tichborne Case,* by Viscount Maugham (1936), pp. 301-303.

during his cross-examination.'

'For how long did you see him?' — 'For about three hours.'

'Did you form your judgment whether he is the Roger Tichborne whom you knew in 1847 and 1848?' — 'I did.'

'What was the judgment?' — 'I could discover nothing that put me in mind of Roger Tichborne.'

'In your judgment and belief, is he or is he not the man?' — 'In my judgment and belief he is not the man.'

Third topic: tattoo marks (notice the orderly and thorough procedure).

'Now, do you remember during the time you were at Stonyhurst with Roger Charles Tichborne, doing anything to either of his arms?' — 'I remember tattooing one of his arms.'

'Which arm was it you tattooed?' — 'The left arm.'

'At the time you tattooed it, was there, or was there not, upon the arm any other tattoo mark then existing?' — 'Yes, there was.'

'What was that then existing mark?' — 'It was a heart, a cross, and an anchor.'

'What was it that you tattooed upon the arm?' — 'I tattooed R.C.T.'

'Will you . . . point out to the jury the position on the arm that you tattooed those initials?' — 'The initials were tattooed about there—about that distance from the wrist . . .'

'Where were the other marks that you have mentioned?'— 'They were above it . . .'

'Now will you tell us how you tattooed it; what materials you used?' — 'Indian ink, and three needles inserted into a small handle of deal.'

'Besides the marks you have just told us, the letters you tattooed, was there any other mark either upon the arm or upon the wrist, so far as you recollect?' — 'There was a small mark on the wrist.'

'What was that small mark on the wrist?' — 'It was probably the result of tattooing, but badly done; it was like a splotch.'

Fourth topic: facts showing that the marks would still be here.

'After you had tattooed the letters you have mentioned, did you see Roger Tichborne's arm bare after you had done it?' — 'Oh, frequently.'

'Up to the time of his leaving Stonyhurst?' — 'Yes.'

'Were the marks you have described to us, including what you put on his arm yourself, still remaining there the last time you saw his arm?' — 'They were.'

'Now, at or about the time you tattooed Roger Charles Tichborne, was there anything done with your arm, or to your arm?' — 'At the same time he tattooed an anchor on my arm . . .'

'What materials was that done with?' — 'With the same material and the same instruments.'

'The same material and the same instruments; the same ink?' — 'The same ink.'

'Have you that mark remaining on your arm now?' — 'I have . . .'

'. . . The mark which you have shown to the jury was done on the same day, with the same instruments, and with the same ink?' — 'It was; probably during the same hour.'

Treating a witness as hostile

If a witness proves to be *hostile* to the party who called him — as distinct from merely being awkward — the court may give leave to that party to treat him as hostile, i.e. to cross-examine him. The main advantages are that he can be asked leading questions point blank, and can be contradicted by means of the proof of his evidence. The curious will find a good example in the *The Trial of Ley and Smith,* [27] where the secretary of the prisoner Ley, being called by the prosecution, proved to have a marked bias in the prisoner's favour, and Lord Goddard gave the prosecution leave to cross-examine her.

[27]   *Op. cit.* p. 119.

Chapter 4

Cross-Examination: Its Aims and Limitations

1 The aims of cross-examination

Testing the evidence-in-chief

A distinguished judge has said:[28]

> 'Cross-examination is a powerful and valuable weapon for the purpose of testing the veracity of a witness and the accuracy and completeness of his story.'

If we compare the evidence-in-chief to a rope — quite strong to all appearances — cross-examination may be compared to the testing of the rope, inch by inch and strand by strand. If the rope is really strong, it will stand the test: if it is weak it will give way at one point or another. It follows that cross-examination ought not to be expected to shake a story which is substantially true.

That is only a picture, but it can with advantage be elaborated a little. For instance, the rope may be stretched out in a new direction; or it may weaken and become slack

---

[28] Lord Hanworth, M.R., quoted with approval by Viscount Sankey, L.C., in *Mechanical etc. Co. Ltd. v Austin* [1935] AC. 346 at p. 359.

under the strain applied to it, without actually breaking; or, finally, the supports which hold it up may give way, with the result that the rope falls to the ground.

Testing the evidence is therefore the keynote of cross-examination: and it will be realised that, quite apart from assisting the party who is conducting the cross-examination, the subjection of evidence to such a test enables the judge to assess its value, and so serves an important public purpose in the administration of justice.

Four specific aims

In greater detail, the aims of cross-examination are these:

(i)   To *destroy* the material parts of the evidence-in-chief;

(ii)   To *weaken* the evidence, where it cannot be destroyed;

(iii)   To *elicit new evidence,* helpful to the party cross-examining; and

(iv)   To *undermine* the witness (or shake his credit, as it is commonly expressed) by showing that he cannot be trusted to speak the truth, or that he is deposing (however honestly) to matters of which he has no real knowledge.

To *destroy* adverse evidence outright is usually too much to hope for, except in rare cases such as the Oscar Wilde trial, or in the cross-examination of a prisoner who has put forward an improbable story. The ideal to be aimed at is to lead the witness to admit that his evidence was untruthful or mistaken. There is an amusing example in the Gladstone libel case where the plaintiff, Captain Wright, had maintained that a certain Cecil Gladstone was the illegitimate son of the famous nineteenth century statesman.[29] Sir Norman Birkett, K.C. (later Lord Birkett)

[29]   See Bowker, *Behind the Bar,* p.175.

produced a reference book which showed the true facts, viz. that Cecil was the lawful son of the statesman's cousin; and putting this into the plaintiff's hands, he said to him:

'Do you still say that Cecil was the illegitimate son of Gladstone?'

'No — not now.'

Such a striking result was made possible by a combination of strong documentary evidence and an honest witness.

The evidence of a witness may also be destroyed if he is driven into a 'pregnant silence' — as where a prisoner, offering a fantastic story, is pressed to explain detail after detail until finally his invention runs out. Familiar examples occur when the prisoner is found in possession of the weapon with which a murder was committed, or of house-breaking implements, or where a witness is cross-examined with the help of incriminating letters.

Yet a third method of destruction is to draw from the witness admissions of facts which are inconsistent with his story, or to draw from him positive assertions of facts which can be disproved. An illustration is again provided by Sir Norman Birkett, in his cross-examination of a taxi-driver who said that he had been driving 'quite slowly'.[30] After tying him down to this statement, Sir Norman obtained, one by one, admissions that ('still going quite slowly') he had (1) drawn out to overtake another vehicle (2) skidded (3) mounted the pavement (4) smashed a plate-glass window (5) knocked over some stalls (6) knocked over three persons and finally (7) knocked over a lamp-post.

In most cases, the objective is not so much to destroy the evidence outright, as to *weaken* it, that is to say to reduce the weight of the evidence and qualify the inferences which might be drawn from it. It is nearly always possible to weaken evidence, and this objective is particularly important where the evidence is circumstantial, so that its damaging effect depends not so much on what is actually

[30]   *Bowker, op. cit.*, p. 95.

said as on what may be deduced from it. The witness may be induced to admit that other explanations are possible; or relentless probing into the details — as in cases where identification is in issue — may show that there is a possibility of a mistake. In this connection, the weaknesses referred to in Chapter 2 under the heading of the fallacies of testimony must be remembered.

The *eliciting of fresh evidence* may lead to a new topic altogether, for instance counsel for the prisoner in a criminal case may be able to use one of the prosecution witnesses to help him to build up an alibi. More often, however, the new evidence simply consists of facts which put a new colour on the evidence-in-chief. If this is done successfully, the result is not only to help in the building up of one's own case, but also, at the same time, to weaken the other side.

Undermining — if successful — destroys the assumptions on which the reliability of the evidence depends. Thus it may be shown that the witness is a confirmed liar, or that he was quite deaf, and could not possibly have heard (except in his imagination) the conversation which he has related with so much assurance.

There are, then, these four main objectives in cross-examination. Here we are simply concerned to point out the results aimed at, and not the methods by which they are reached, as the *technique* of cross-examination is the subject of the next chapter. To anticipate a little, however, it must be stated at once that particular techniques do not necessarily coincide with particular objectives: there is not, for instance, one technique for destruction, and another for weakening, but the same technique may be used for different purposes according to the nature of the case, or it may be used for more than one purpose at the same time. The varying uses of each technique are set out in the next chapter, as each technique in turn is explained and illustrated.

Two important rules of practice

The foregoing paragraphs set out the *practical* objectives of cross-examination. There are, besides, two rules of practice, firmly established in British courts, which must be complied with.

The first is that *the witness must be cross-examined on all material facts which are disputed.* Otherwise the court will take it that his evidence is not contested.

The second rule is that *an advocate, in cross-examining, must put to the witness the case he is going to set up,* so far as it lies within the witness's knowledge: such cross-examination is a necessary preliminary to the calling of contradictory evidence.

Some quite well-known advocates seem to look upon cross-examination as little more than a formal compliance with these rules, 'suggesting' to the witness that he is mistaken about this, that and the other, and 'putting it to him' that the facts set up on the other side are true. This procedure has at any rate the merit of 'obtaining denials' and so showing precisely what is in issue. A real artist, however, will comply with the rule that he must challenge the adverse evidence not in any perfunctory and formal manner, but by using all the resources of his technique to weaken, undermine or destroy it. Likewise, instead of formally putting his case to obtain denials, he will try to insinuate it and build it up out of the witness's own mouth. Sometimes, of course, there is no scope for anything but a formal challenge.

Because of the rule that adverse evidence must be challenged, there is no place in British courts for the so-called 'silent' cross-examination which is favoured in the United States in appropriate cases.

2 The limits of cross-examination

What questions are allowed under the law of evidence

This question is answered fully in the text-books on the law of evidence, but the outlines of the subject are sketched in here because of their practical bearing.

Cross-examination is not allowed to roam at large over every subject under the sun. Questions are not allowed unless either (i) they are relevant to the issues in the case, or (ii) though relating to collateral questions, they tend to impeach the credit of the witness (i.e. to undermine him).

So far as questions are relevant to the issues, they are governed by the ordinary rules on the admissibility of evidence. Hearsay, for example, is not in strict theory admissible. In practice, it is true, great latitude is allowed in cross-examining as to conversations and matters of that kind. If, however, a particular question is objected to as introducing hearsay evidence, the cross-examiner must be prepared to justify the evidence on one or other of the recognised grounds: for example that it is an admission made by the opposite party, or a statement made in his presence, or a statement which accompanied and explained the *res gestae*. When cross-examining counsel introduces part of a conversation or statement in this way, the whole of the conversation or statement becomes admissible in re-examination.

Questions directed to credit are designed to show that the evidence of the witness cannot be trusted: for instance they may be directed to such matters as bias, previous inconsistent statements, and previous character, conduct and convictions tending to show that he is a liar or generally dishonest. In general, evidence cannot be given afterwards (by the party cross-examining) to prove matters which the witness denies, but, exceptionally, contradictory evidence is allowed to prove bias or hostility, previous inconsistent statement, previous convictions, or a general reputation for untruthfulness. Two of these cases are governed by special statutory provisions, which are summarised below:

(i) Previous inconsistent statements[31]

The witness should be reminded of the circumstances in which he made such a statement, and then asked whether he made it. If the statement was in writing, his attention must be called to the relevant part. If, after these preliminaries, the witness does not distinctly admit that he made the statement, evidence may be called — in due course — to contradict him. The most frequent case arises when the depositions in a criminal case are brought up to challenge a prosecution witness. The preliminary questions run something like this:

'Did you given evidence before the justices?' — 'Yes.'

'Was your evidence taken down?' — 'Yes.'

'And read over to you?' — 'Yes.'

'And did you sign it?' — 'Yes.'

'Look at the depositions. Is that your signature?' — 'Yes.'

'And did you say in your evidence (whatever it may be)?'

Here, the witness having admitted the statement, there will be no need to prove it independently.

(ii) Previous convictions[32]

A witness may be asked whether he has been convicted of any felony or misdemeanour, and if he does not admit the conviction, it may be proved by an official certificate under s. 73 of the Police and Criminal Evidence Act 1984.

---

[31]   Criminal Procedure Act 1865, ss. 4, 5.

[32]   Criminal Procedure Act, 1865, s. 6.

The use of documents in cross-examination[33]

A witness may be cross-examined as to whether he made a statement contained in a document without, in the first instance, showing it to him; but the document (or the material part of it) must be shown to the witness if he denies that he signed it, and if evidence is thereafter to be called to contradict him. Cross-examining on a part of a document, it should be noted, may make the whole of it admissible in evidence. On the other hand, while a witness may be asked whether he wrote or signed a document without the necessity for showing it to him, he cannot be asked questions as to the contents of a document (such as what he meant by a certain phrase, or why he wrote it) until the document is properly put in as evidence. This distinction between cross-examination as the *making* of a written statement, and cross-examination as to its *contents,* is a cardinal one in the law of cross-examination on documents.

An alternative procedure is to put the document in the hands of the witness — without proving it, reading it out or putting it in evidence — and asking him:

'Now, after looking at that document, do you still adhere to what you said before?'

(See the illustration from the Gladstone libel case, quoted on pp. 50-1, *ante*.)

This procedure is useful where the cross-examining counsel does not wish to put the document in evidence, or where it will be difficult to prove it.

---

[33]   See F. J. Wrottesley, K.C. (later Wrottesley, L.J.) *Examination of Witnesses* (2nd ed.), pp. 65-70, where there are some illuminating notes.

Cross-examining the defendant in a criminal case

The Criminal Evidence Act, 1898, which gave to defendants in criminal cases the privilege of giving evidence on their own behalf, also contained safeguards to ensure that a defendant who gave evidence would not be treated oppressively. An accused person who gives evidence cannot be asked any question tending to show that he has committed, or been convicted of, or charged with, any other offence, or that he is of bad character, unless:

(i)   he has set up his own good character as part of his case; or

(ii)   he has attacked the character of the prosecutor or the prosecution witnesses; or

(iii)   he has given evidence against a co-defendant charged with the same offence.

These restrictions are intended to prohibit *cross-examination to credit,* directed to character or previous convictions. In those exceptional cases where previous offences of the same kind ('similar facts') are admissible in evidence to prove system or intent, evidence of the previous offences is offered by the prosecution and the Act expressly provides (section 1(f) (i)) that the prisoner may be cross-examined thereon.

Nothing in the Criminal Evidence Act, 1898, makes a question admissible where it would not have been admissible before: thus to ask the prisoner whether he has been *charged* with a previous offence — but acquitted — is not in general relevant either to the issues in the case or to credit, and such a question must usually be disallowed: *Maxwell v. Director of Public Prosecutions* [1935] A.C. 309.

Reserve power of the court

The judge has power to disallow irrelevant questions and wasteful repetition but should be slow to override counsel's discretion: *Jones v. N.C.B.* [1957] 2 All E.R. 155.

In the Tichborne case, Coleridge cross-examined some of the witnesses at great length and with many repetitions, which drew some courteous criticism from the judge.[34] Viscount Maugham, in writing about this case, has expressed the opinion that where the volume of material is considerable, it is the duty of counsel to make a selection of the points which are really important.[35] A cross-examination about *minutiae* can go on for ever. Another Lord Chancellor, in an appeal in the House of Lords, has said:[36]

> '. . . protracted and irrelevant cross-examination not only adds to the cost of litigation but is a waste of public time.'

Neither of these great authorities would deny that length is sometimes inevitable. In the average case, however, cross-examination can, and should, be kept within reasonable limits.

The ethics of cross-examination

The abuse of cross-examination was the subject of extensive controversy during the nineteenth century, when, in the absence of world wars and atom bombs, cross-examination in court was one of the most unpleasant hazards which could disturb the settled life of the ordinary citizen. Thus in the middle of the century Archbishop Whately, a scholar of some repute at the time, though now

---

34   *Op. cit.,* pp. 231-234.
35   *Op. cit.,* p. 145.
36   *Mechanical etc. Co. Ltd. v. Austin* [1935] A.C. 346, per Viscount Sankey, L.C., at p. 360.

forgotten, criticised the bar on the ground that they frequently bullied witnesses. Towards the end of the century, Sir Charles Russell, Q.C. (the first Lord Russell of Killowen) was criticised for the severe way in which he attacked the credit of a witness. There may have been some justification for these criticisms. It is certainly noticeable that during the last fifty years the style of cross-examination has become more quiet and (in appearance) less formidable: and while the gentle manner of such distinguished advocates as Sir Norman Birkett and Sir Roland Oliver produced first-class results, it is doubtful whether either would be feared, as witnesses feared Russell or Carson. The truth is that gentleness and firmness both have their place, according to the type of case and the reactions of the witness, and further, that it is possible to be firm without being dominating.[37]

A much more important matter is the use of cross-examination to attack the character of a witness. Not very long ago, a judge criticised counsel for attacking the character of a witness (on matters directly in issue) without afterwards calling evidence to substantiate the allegations. The Code of Conduct for the English Bar (1990) contains the following instructions for avoiding such abuses:

A practising barrister when conducting proceedings at Court:

(e) must not make statements or ask questions which are merely scandalous or intended or calculated only to vilify insult or annoy either a witness or some other person;

(f) must if possible avoid the naming in open Court of third parties whose character would thereby be impugned;

(g) must not by assertion in a speech impugn a witness whom he has had an opportunity to cross-examine unless in cross-examination he has given the witness an opportunity to answer the allegation;

[37] There is an amusing caricature in Walt Disney's film, *Ichabod and Mr. Toad,* of the 'browbeating' type of counsel who is now rarely encountered.

(h) must not suggest that a witness or other person is guilty of crime fraud or misconduct or attribute to another person the crime or conduct of which his lay client is accused unless such allegations go to a matter in issue (including the credibility of the witness) which is material to his lay client's case and which appear to him to be supported by reasonable grounds.

The practical limits of cross-examination

Cross-examination is overrated in popular belief, as if, like the waving of a magician's, wand, it could succeed by itself in winning a hopeless case. Now cross-examination may always bring out weaknesses, but these may not be decisive. The destructive cross-examination, which shatters a whole case at one stroke, is a rare phenomenon. Perhaps the most outstanding case of this sort in modern times was the case of Oscar Wilde, and it is worth seeing exactly what happened. Oscar Wilde, the dramatist, was accused by Lord Queensberry of 'posing' as a man who engaged in homosexual practices (a very serious accusation in the 19th century), and brought a criminal prosecution for libel to vindicate himself. Carson, in cross-examining Wilde, confronted him with a whole series of facts showing that the libel was true, and finally Wilde broke down under this pressure. (The substance of this cross-examination is reproduced in the next chapter.) But the case did not terminate there and then: it was not until Carson had made his speech for the defence, and announced his intention of calling a damaging witness whose presence had not been suspected, that the prosecution withdrew their charges and submitted to a verdict. This illustration shows that even the most devastating cross-examination is only one factor in advocacy. The presence of witnesses to support the cross-examination with affirmative evidence is usually essential. It is noteworthy that Carson's cross-examination did not appear from nowhere, but was based on painstaking inquiries by detectives: and the same feature can be traced in other famous cases.[38-9]

Dangers in carrying cross-examination too far

There are certain practical risks in carrying cross-examination too far, which it is convenient to mention at this point. These are as follows:

(i) The 'dangerous' question.

A really critical question — one which may decide the case adversely — should not be asked unless the answer is known. That does not mean that critical points must be avoided. The proper course is to approach them very cautiously, little by little, thus gaining some idea of what the answer is likely to be.[40-1] Sometimes the taking of a risk becomes unavoidable, but it should always be a carefully calculated risk, not one which is taken blindly.

(ii) The 'unnecessary' question

This is a rather similar matter. When good results have been obtained, it is always possible that by a question intended to clinch the matter, the whole effect may be

---

[38-9] E.g. Sir John Simon's cross-examination of Robinson in *The Mr. A. Case,* part of which is quoted on pp. 101, 108, *post.*

[40-1] See an example at p. 94, *post:* also the remarks of Sir Henry Curtis-Bennett, quoted in *Curtis,* p. 224. An illustration of the neglect of conscious technique is provided by the fact that Curtis-Bennett (like some other contemporary advocates) appears to suggest that cross-examination has no other technique than the avoidance of the 'dangerous' or 'unnecessary' question. Chapter 5 shows clearly that this is a superficial view.

spoilt. If the cross-examiner has got ninety per cent of what he wanted, he should usually stop, because further questions may produce an unexpected explanation which tells against him.

(iii) Making evidence admissible

If a conversation or document was inadmissible as evidence-in-chief, cross-examination on part of it may make the whole of it admissible, perhaps with very damaging results. Similarly in a criminal case a reckless attack on the character of the prosecution witnesses in cross-examination may open the way to a damaging cross-examination of the prisoner on his own character and previous convictions.

Cross-Examination: Its Technique

1 Preliminary

In this chapter we reach the heart of the subject of cross-examination, namely, its technique. Viscount Maugham writes:[42]

> 'Many a counsel has risen to his feet wishing that the system of cross-examination had never been invented. He must ask something, but what? Many counsel content themselves with asking over again a few of the questions which have already been asked, and then sitting down, avoiding if possible a sigh of relief.'

The objectives are clear enough, and have already been explained: to destroy, to weaken, to elicit fresh evidence, to undermine. Here we turn to the difficult question: How?

The conclusions which follow are based on a great mass of material, published and unpublished. A number of illustrations have been included, but considerations of space have made it necessary to select specimens which are reasonably short.

---

[42] *The Tichborne Case,* p. 303. Lord Maugham is referring to the special case of a witness who is known to be telling the truth, but the comment has general application.

As in examination-in-chief, a prerequisite of success is a clear picture of the case as a whole. By this means, as the evidence-in-chief is elicited, it will be easy to see how much can be admitted and how much has to be challenged, also how far the witness has knowledge of other matters which can be used to build up an affirmative case in one's own favour. Further, again as in examination-in-chief, skill in asking simple and clear questions is indispensable.

In general, it is no use going over the story which has been told already by the witness, merely in the hope that with insistence and pressure the story will be altered. This is likely to make the evidence stronger, rather than weaken it. It is necessary to tackle the witness from a new angle, and adopt a strategy of indirect approach.

Subject to these remarks, cross-examination should be thorough, in that it should test every part of the story which is contested. Thoroughness is not the same thing as lengthiness, and long cross-examinations with unnecessary repetitions are bad technique. On the other hand cross-examination — unlike examination-in-chief — certainly need not follow chronological order, though it ought to follow some pre-arranged plan, and is often arranged according to different topics. Wrottesley, L.J., says:[43]

> 'Except . . . where you have a definite reason for doing otherwise, let your cross-examination proceed in order of date, or arranged into topics or somehow logically, as the nature of the case may demand.'

He adds that if the witness is 'a deliberate and calculating liar', that is a good reason for departing from a settled order. However, the *arrangement* of cross-examination is considered in the next chapter, while here we are concerned more with the development of particular techniques, and it is only necessary to say that cross-examination should be *orderly,* though in a looser way than examination-in-chief.

---

[43]   *Letters to a Young Barrister,* pp. 60, 62.

The principles of clearness, thoroughness and orderliness ought to permeate the whole texture of cross-examination, whatever particular technique is for the moment being employed.

2 The main techniques

Successful cross-examination is founded on three main techniques: confrontation, probing, and insinuation — or rather two techniques, probing and insinuation, because confrontation is only firm insinuation on a massive scale, but it is convenient to treat it separately because it has featured prominently in celebrated cases.

Confrontation, as the name indicates, consists of confronting the witness with a great mass of damaging facts which he cannot deny and which are inconsistent with his evidence. It is a destructive technique, but when it fails to destroy it may still succeed in weakening. It cannot be employed in a massive way unless there is strong material at the service of the cross-examiner: consequently it tends to be prominent in big cases of rather an unusual character, especially big libel actions where there has been the opportunity to carry out investigations and collect damaging material. Nevertheless, quite a small number of indisputable facts — even one incriminating letter — may be used to great advantage in ordinary cases. This is the everyday technique of firm insinuation.

Probing consists of inquiring thoroughly into the details of the story to discover flaws. It may be used either to weaken or destroy, or open up a lead to something new.

Insinuation is a many-sided technique, and is perhaps the most important of the three in everyday practice. In essence, it is the building-up of a different version of the evidence-in-chief, by bringing out new facts and possibilities, so that, while helping to establish a positive case in one's own favour, at the same time it weakens the evidence-in-chief by drawing out its sting. Insinuation may take the form of quietly leading the witness on, little by little: alternatively it may be necessary to drive him, and in that case, as in confrontation, the cross-examiner must have material at his disposal. (In fact, confrontation is here used in aid of insinuation.) Thus there are two main forms of the technique, gentle insinuation and firm insinuation.

It would be wrong to think of these various techniques as wholly distinct. They may be closely associated together, or there may be a swift transition from one form to another. Probing, for instance, may disclose a weak point which suggests a line for insinuation: or it may lead the witness to make statements which can be destroyed by confrontation. Again, when a witness is confronted with an incriminating letter, this is always followed up by probing into the meaning of the statements in the letter. Yet again, gentle insinuation may become firmer, if the witness is difficult to lead.

There is also a fourth line of approach, which may be called *the technique of undermining*. This is not a separate technique, since it uses the methods of the other two, but it uses them for a totally different purpose: its object is not to break down the evidence by inquiring into the facts, but to take away the foundations of the evidence by showing that either (i) the witness does not know what he is talking about, or (ii) if he does know the truth, he cannot be trusted to tell it. In other words, it is the same thing as cross-examination to credit, but to call it undermining brings out its true nature more clearly.

3 The technique of confrontation

Confrontation consists of firing damaging facts at the witness to break down his story. These facts may have been assembled specially for use in cross-examination, but more commonly they are taken from the general body of evidence collected to fight the case, and have either been proved already, or will be proved in due course.

There is a good illustration of confrontation in its simplest form in the American case of the Eno will.[44] Columbia University were the residuary legatees under the will of Amos R. Eno, which was contested by his two nephews. A lady gave evidence that the testator, in conversation with her, had expressed great admiration for Columbia University, and that in a later conversation he had praised a friend of his who made a university his residuary legatee. In cross-examination she was confronted with the fact that the testator had made several wills since these conversations, and that in none of them was there any bequest to Columbia University. In the same case another witness gave evidence that he had talked to the testator in the smoking car of a railway train, and found him in full possession of his faculties. This witness was confronted, among other things, with the fact that the testator never smoked and hated the odour of tobacco — so much so that he left his guests at his own dinner-parties when the time arrived for them to light their cigars.

Confrontation appears in its most massive form when there are a large number of facts or documents — especially documents — to be used against the witness. These facts are put to the witness one at a time, and he is drawn on to give explanations, which may be destroyed by producing something more. The tendency is to start with the least damaging points, and to reserve the most effective to give the finishing stroke. The cross-examination of Oscar Wilde by Sir Edward Carson, Q.C. (later Lord Carson) was a brilliant example of this technique. As, by general consent, Carson was the outstanding cross-examiner of modern times, this is worth quoting at length. The background of

---

[44]   See Francis L. Wellman, *The Art of Cross-examination* (1923) pp. 71-75.

this case was as follows.[45] Oscar Wilde, a leading author and playwright of the late nineteenth century, was accused by Lord Queensberry of 'posing as a sodomite' — i.e. a man addicted to unnatural practices with other male persons. In order to vindicate himself, he commenced a prosecution for criminal libel against Lord Queensberry — an unwise step, as it turned out, because the imputation was true. Wilde stated in evidence that there was no truth in the suggestions that he was guilty of unnatural offences, or approved of such conduct. Now Carson had evidence of (1) Wilde's books, some of which might convey immoral implications; (2) personal letters; and (3) actual association with a series of young men for immoral purposes. He used his facts in that order. But by way of an opening gambit he confronted Wilde with the true facts as to his age, which Wilde had understated, and thus at the very start caught him out in a lie.

'You stated that your age was thirty-nine. I think you are over forty. You were born on 16th October, 1854?' —

'I have no wish to pose as being young. I am thirty-nine or forty. You have my certificate and that settles the matter.'

'But being born in 1854 makes you more that forty?' —

'Ah! very well.'

After a number of subsidiary matters, Carson started quoting passages from Wilde's books. He read out from a novel, *The Picture of Dorian Gray,* a long passage describing a meeting between an artist and a young man, Dorian Gray, to whom he was greatly attracted. The following brief extracts give all that is necessary to understand the cross-examination.

'I turned halfway round, and saw Dorian Gray for the first time . . . I knew that I had come face to face with someone whose mere personality was so fascinating that, if I allowed

[45]   *The Trials of Oscar Wilde,* ed. H. Montgomery Hyde (1948), cross-examination at pp. 120-152. Owing to the peculiar nature of the case I have hesitated to use this example, but cannot find a better one.

it to do so, it would absorb my whole nature, my whole soul, my very art itself . . . I couldn't be happy if I didn't see him every day . . . a few minutes with somebody one worships means a great deal . . .'

Carson continued:

'Now I ask you, Mr. Wilde, do you consider that the description of the feeling of one man towards a youth just grown up was a proper or an improper feeling?' —

'I think it is the most perfect description of what an artist would feel on meeting a beautiful personality that was in some way necessary to his art and life.'

Then after reading a similar passage:

'Do you mean to say that that passage describes the natural feeling of one man towards another?' — 'It would be the influence produced by a beautiful personality.'

'May I take it that you, as an artist, have never known the feeling described here?' — 'I have never allowed any personality to dominate my art.'

'Then you have never known the feeling you described?' — 'No. It is a work of fiction . . .'

'But let us go over it phrase by phrase. "I quite admit that I adored you madly . . ." Have you ever adored a young man madly?' — 'No, not madly . . .'

'. . . "I was jealous of every one to whom you spoke." Have you ever been jealous of a young man?' — 'Never in my life.'

' "I wanted to have you all to myself." Did you ever have that feeling?' — 'No: I should consider it an intense nuisance, an intense bore . . .'

So far so good: Wilde denied that the passages had any personal bearing, but was tied down to the explanation that he was only concerned, as an artist, to portray life as it was, with strange as well as normal manifestations. This would not do to explain things with a more personal bearing: Carson now brought to bear private letters addressed to Wilde's friend Lord Alfred Douglas, the style of which appears from these extracts:

'Dearest of all Boys,

'Your letter was delightful . . . but I am sad and out of sorts . . . Why are you not here, my dear, my wonderful boy? . . .

Your own Oscar.'

Carson asked:

'Is that an ordinary letter?' — 'Everything I write is extraordinary. I do not pose as being ordinary. . .'

'Is it the kind of letter a man writes to another?' — 'It was a tender expression of my great admiration for Lord Alfred Douglas. It was not, like the other, a prose poem.'

Already, it will be noted, Wilde was being forced away from the 'literary' explanation of his peculiar style. There followed the most damaging facts of all: Wilde was confronted with his association with a series of young men, all of humble origin, to all of whom he had paid money. For instance:

'. . . did Taylor introduce you to Charles Parker?' — 'Yes.'

'Did you become friendly with him?' — 'Yes, he was one with whom I became friendly.'

'Did you know that Parker was a gentleman's servant out of employment?' — 'No . . .'

'How old was he?' — 'Really, I do not keep a census.'

'Never mind about a census. Tell me how old he was?' — 'I should say he was about twenty. He was young and that was one of his attractions.'

'Was he a literary character?' — 'Oh, no.'

'Was he intellectual?' — 'Culture was not his strong point. He was not an artist . . .'

'How much money did you give Parker?' — '. . . I should think £4 or £5.'

'Why?' — 'Because he was poor, and I liked him . . .'

The talk of 'art' and 'literature' was now wearing very thin.

Finally, the finishing stroke was given by a surprise attack.

'Do you know Walter Grainger?' — 'Yes.'

'How old is he?' — 'He was about sixteen when I knew him . . .'

And here is the surprise — a sudden question from a totally unexpected angle —

> 'Did you ever kiss him?' — 'Oh, dear no . . . He was, unfortunately, extremely ugly . . .'
>
> 'Was that the reason why you did not kiss him?' — 'Oh, Mr. Carson, you are pertinently insolent.'
>
> 'Did you say that in support of your statement that you never kissed him?' — 'No. It is a childish question . . .'
>
> 'Why did you mention his ugliness?' — 'It is ridiculous to imagine that any such thing could have occurred under any circumstances.'
>
> 'Then why did you mention his ugliness, I ask you?' — 'Perhaps because you insulted me by an insulting question.'
>
> 'Was that a reason why you should say the boy was ugly.?'
>
> (At this point the witness became inarticulate and unable to answer.)

This was, of course, a most exceptional type of case. It illustrates clearly the use of confrontation in bringing out one point at a time, tying the witness down to explanations, and then confronting him with further facts which shatter his explanations.[46] The technique is at its best when it is necessary to expose a deliberate liar, and plenty of evidence is available, especially in the form of incriminating letters. It is used frequently against the prisoner in a criminal case.

Here, however, is a good illustration of the everyday use of confrontation (in its reduced form of firm insinuation) to establish a *small* point in a case. It is from *The Mr. A. Case,*[47] and Sir John Simon is cross-examining Mr.

---

[46] Further examples, too long to quote, even in an abbreviated form, may be found in Sir Thomas Inskip's cross-examination of Bywaters in *The Trial of Bywaters and Thompson,* ed. Filson Young (1923) at pp. 56-73; and Sir Charles Russell's cross-examination of Pigott regarding the forged Parnell letters, quoted in Wellman, *op. cit.,* pp. 263-276.

[47] *Op. cit.,* p. 58.

Robinson with a view to showing that he had no means of his own at a certain date.

'What did you go bankrupt for if you had got any money?' — 'One can be forced into bankruptcy without that.'

'. . . I have here the Official Receiver's report . . . Is this right: No assets were disclosed by the bankrupt? You were the bankrupt?' — 'Yes.'

'Is it true that you did not disclose that you had a sixpence?' — 'I had nothing to disclose apparently.'

Here the production of the official Report and the skilful use made of it resulted in the swift destruction of the witness's evasion.

In the Wilde case, Carson was in a position to destroy the evidence-in-chief as it stood, i.e. Wilde's denial of immoral conduct. In other cases it might be necessary to lead the witness on to something further before confronting him with the evidence. Thus when Sir Charles Russell, Q.C., was questioning Pigott, who had forged certain letters implicating a Member of Parliament in a terrorist plot, he first of all asked him to write down a number of words, one of which was the word 'hesitancy', spelt by the witness as 'hesitency'. This word had been spelt in this way in one of the forged letters, which in due course was to be produced to destroy Pigott. Such tactics may be described as 'leading the witness on'. Again, it is possible that the witness will be evasive: he is almost certain to be, if he is telling a false story, but has a vague idea that there are documents which can be brought up against him. In such a case it is necessary, in the first instance, to pin the witness down to precise admissions and denials, in order to prevent him from wriggling out of the net. There is a good example in Sir Patrick Hastings' cross-examination of Professor Laski, quoted at p. 106, *post*.

So much for confrontation. To summarise the scope of this technique:

(i)   It should not be used without strong material, preferably facts which the witness cannot deny.

(ii)   The facts should be put one at a time.

(iii)   As soon as each fact is put and admitted, all its damaging implications should be drawn out one by one.

(iv)   If the witness offers lame explanations, he should be pinned down to them precisely.

(v)   The other facts are then put in turn, in such a way as to demolish the explanations.

(vi)   The aim is to force the witness to admit the falsity of his story; or to make him tongue-tied; or to involve him in contradictions.

4 The technique of probing

The technique of probing has this marked advantage over confrontation, that it can be used without having any material for cross-examination: for it consists simply in delving into the story as told, so as to detect and expose its inherent weaknesses. The characteristic of probing is to ask such questions as Who? What? Where? When? Why? — and more particularly Why?[48]

But though all probing consists of delving into the detailed facts, this may be done for several different reasons. If — as in identification — it is believed that the witness has interpreted the facts wrongly, the object will be to

---

[48]   It is interesting to note that Quintilian, the leading Roman authority on oratory, recognised the difference between the two techniques of confrontation and probing, for after referring to the importance of amassing material and its use in asking questions he goes on to say that, even without material, it is possible to interrogate witnesses about antecedents, consequences, persons and places: *Institutes of Oratory,* Book V, Chap. 7. Later there is a reference to the typical procedure of insinuation — approaching a subject cautiously, step by step.

investigate the grounds of his statement. If the story is believed to be false, the object may be to draw the witness on until he asserts a fact which can be contradicted: alternatively he may be asked searching questions about things he claims to have seen until his invention runs out or he makes improbable statements. This list is not exhaustive.

There is no field of advocacy in which practical judgment — the flair for detecting a weak point — is more valuable. Because of the remarkable gift which Hawkins had in this direction, it is probable that, in the technique of probing, he remains unexcelled.

It has already been pointed out that probing is used as an auxiliary to confrontation: where a passage in a letter has been put to the witness, the cross-examiner will probe into the detailed implications of the passage. Probing may also be used as the starting-point for insinuation, that is to say a little preliminary probing may indicate an approach by which favourable facts can be established. In itself, however, probing is a destructive technique: it seeks to destroy, or failing that, to weaken.

As an introductory illustration, here is an extract from *The Trial of Roger Casement* (for high treason).[49] Serjeant Sullivan, K.C., is cross-examining an Irish peasant, John McCarthy, who deposed to going out in the early hours of the morning and finding an abandoned boat and footprints. The cross-examination did not help Serjeant Sullivan a great deal — his object seems to be to show improbability — but it is a good specimen of the general style of probing, and is, besides, entertaining.

'Do you usually get up at 2 o'clock in the morning?' — 'No.'

'Or had you been to bed at all?' — 'Yes'

'Then you got up this morning at 2 o'clock in the morning?' — 'Yes.'

[49]   Ed. G. H. Knott (Hodge, 1917), p. 45.

'What got you up so early?' — 'I went to a well.'

'Thirsty?' — 'No.'

'What brought you to the well?' — 'Saying a few prayers.'

The Attorney-General, interposing: 'It was Good Friday morning, it being a holy well.'

Sjt. Sullivan. 'Being Good Friday morning, did you say it is a holy well?' — 'I heard the old people saying it was.'

'Were you ever saying your prayers at the well before?' — 'No.'

'Is it a long way from your house?' — 'Over a mile.'

'A dark night; a pretty dark night, was it not?' — 'It was when I was leaving.'

'You left in the dark, having got up at 2 o'clock in the morning to say prayers at a well you have never been to before?'— 'Yes.'

'What is the name of the well?' — 'It is an Irish well; I could not think of it.'

'If it is an Irish name you ought to think of it all the sooner, though we are in a strange country.' — 'I have not the Irish.'

'You have not the Irish, but . . . what is the name of the place it is at?' — 'Ballyprior.'

'You did not meet anybody at this well at 2 o'clock in the morning?' — 'No.'

'Nobody else was out on Good Friday morning at 2 o'clock saying prayers at the holy well; is not that so?' — 'That is so.'

Notice how Sullivan insists on his questions being answered and allows no evasion.

Turning now to the specific matters which may be made the subject of probing, we find that they can be grouped conveniently under four main headings:

(i)   The basis of a complex fact, such as identification, or the conclusions of an expert.

(ii) Antecedents.

(iii) Consequences.

(iv) Collateral circumstances — especially time, place, and persons, and their descriptions.

(i) Probing into the foundations of a statement: mistaken interpretation

Many things which are stated by witnesses as if they were quite simple and positive facts are, in reality, based on a more complex foundation which consists partly of observed facts and partly of theories and preconceptions: in short, they are not observations, but interpretations. Attention was drawn to this phenomenon in Chapter 2 (pp. 27-9, *ante*), which forms the theoretical background of this section and should be read in conjunction with it. Illustrations may be found in such statements as this: 'X was drunk'; 'X did not know of the existence of a will'; 'X suffered from heart attacks'; 'I saw X near the scene of the crime.'

Every statement of fact should therefore be analysed to see how far it is based on underlying facts and assumptions, and, if so, to see whether these facts and assumptions can be shaken. An important case, which is always recurring in practice, is the question of identification. The extracts which follow are taken from the Tichborne case.[50] Col. Norbury, who had known the original Roger Tichborne as an officer in his regiment, had testified that the claimant who had arrived from Australia was the same man. This is how Hawkins probed into his statement:

'Is there any particular feature in the face which you can point out as having remembered in Roger Tichborne . . .?' — '. . . I remember a peculiar working upwards of the eyebrows and the wrinkles across his forehead . . .'

'Have you seen that in any other people, the working of the eyelids?' — 'I have; no doubt I have . . .'

'Have you seen the same thing in a hundred other people?' — 'Possibly; I cannot say . . .'

'It was not a very extraordinary circumstance?' — 'No, I think not.'

[50]   *Op. cit.,* pp. 172-173.

'Do you remember the colour of his eyes?' — 'No; I do not. I am very bad at the colour of people's eyes.'

'I will try you with the nose — do you recollect the nose?' — 'No, I cannot say that I do.'

'Do you recollect the ears?' — 'No, nothing particular about them.'

'Do you recollect a single feature in the man's face?' — 'I told you his eyebrows and the forehead; that is all.'

'Was he narrow or broad-chested?' — 'I do not think he was remarkably narrow-chested.'

Identification can, of course, be pursued further in such matters as hair (colour, length, style) and voice (including the accent). Failure on the part of the witness to speak to individual features weakens identification, but does not destroy it, as a mere general impression is some evidence, though weak.

The foundations of expert opinion

The foundations of the opinion of an expert can be probed into in much the same way. Such an opinion is founded partly on facts, some of which may have been seen by the expert himself (as where a doctor has taken part in a post-mortem examination), but some of which, almost certainly, are derived from the evidence of other witnesses. It is most important to show how far the expert is relying on facts which can be disputed. The other link in the expert's opinion is the theoretical deductions drawn from the facts, and these also can be probed into, provided that the cross-examiner has taken care to acquire some knowledge of the subject from his own experts. In the Arran case[51] two young men had together climbed Goat Fell in the Isle of Arran: one of them came down alone, and the body of the other was found later on the mountainside with severe head injuries. Dr. Fullarton gave evidence that in his opinion

---

[51] *The Trial of John Watson Laurie,* ed. W. Roughead (1932), pp.123-124.

death was due to repeated blows on the head with a blunt instrument. The defence suggested that death might be due to a fall from a height. Here is an extract from the cross-examination of Dr. Fullarton by J. B. Balfour, Q.C., (later Lord Kinross, and at the time, as Dean of Faculty, the leader of the Scottish bar):

'I think the first reason you gave for the opinion that these injuries resulted from repeated blows was the severity and extent of the lines of fracture?' — 'Severity of the fractures and extent.'

'Let us first take severity. Do you think that, if a person fell over either 19 feet or 32 feet and pitched on to a granite rock, the severity of the blow would not be as great as any inflicted by the hand?' — 'It would be, but it would not cause so many fractures.'

'We will speak about that directly. Would not a sheer fall on the vertex of the head upon a hard object be more severe than a blow from a stone in a man's hand?' — 'It would be, from a sufficient height; but it would end in only one smash. And you cannot compare the severity in that way.'

'Would there be, apart from direction, a kind of proportion between the severity of the blow and the extent of the resulting injuries? Could you imagine anything more likely to shatter a man's head than a fall down a cliff of 19 feet?' — 'I could not, and that is the reason why I think it was due to blows. The injury was localised.'

'Do the lines of fracture you have indicated not implicate the whole of the top of the head?' __ 'Yes.'

Balfour first fixed the two basic facts on which the opinion was based: severity of the fractures, and their extent. He then took these one by one and showed that they were compatible with another interpretation.

(ii) Probing into antecedent facts[52]

In one sense of the words antecedents simply means the facts which, in point of time, occurred before those related

---

[52]   I have been unable to find a good illustration.

in evidence. In attacking a false alibi, for instance, it may be useful to go back in point of time — an hour or a few hours, or perhaps a day — to see whether the alibi fits in with its surroundings.

Antecedents may be followed up in another sense in an endeavour to trace causes or explanations, especially the motives and reasons which led the witness to act in a certain way. 'Why?' is one of the most useful questions in cross-examination, and can be pursued relentlessly, especially in cross-examining a defendant in a criminal case. 'Why were you carrying that gun? Why did you buy poison? Why did you write that letter?' This line of attack does not need to be elaborated.

(iii) Probing into consequences

It is often useful to follow up the consequences of the facts deposed to. There are several variants of this procedure. In such a case as a false alibi, or in any case where it is suspected that the witness was not on the scene at the time stated, it may be useful to trace the sequence of subsequent events to see whether the story fits on to other proved facts. Again, the consequences of the facts deposed to — that is, their natural results — may be developed: in an accident case, it may be possible to develop the sort of damage which would be caused if the accident happened in the manner stated, and to show that in fact the results are different.

Frequently a witness deposes to a certain *state of mind*. It may then be useful to work out what he would have done if that state of mind had been genuine. There is a good illustration in *The Trial of Crippen*.[53] Dr. Crippen's wife had disappeared mysteriously. In response to police inquiries he said that she had eloped with another man, but afterwards he took to flight, and during his absence his

[53] Ed. Filson Young (Hodge, 1920), p. 114.

wife's remains were discovered buried under the floor of his cellar. Medical tests disclosed the presence of poison in the body. It will be seen that, if Dr. Crippen's story was true, he believed that his wife was still alive (and with another man) at the time of his arrest: for he had not been told of the discovery in the cellar. This is how Sir Richard Muir, K.C., in cross-examining the doctor, tested the genuineness of this belief:

> '. . . I realised that I was being arrested for murder.'
>
> 'The murder of your wife?' — 'Yes.'
>
> 'Up to that time did you believe she was alive?' — 'I did.'
>
> 'Did you put any question to Inspector Dew as to whether she had been found?' — 'I did not put any question at all.'
>
> 'As to how he knew she was dead?' — 'No.'
>
> (By the Lord Chief Justice.) 'You put no question at all?' — 'I put no questions at all.'

Finally, it may be helpful to probe into the consequences of a *theory* which has been put forward or suggested by the other side: for instance, if the evidence is that death has been caused in such a way that blood spurted everywhere, what would be the effect on the clothing of the murderer, and what traces would he leave at or near the scene?[54]

(iv) Probing into collateral circumstances

The last heading for the technique of probing is collateral circumstances, of which the most obvious are those quoted by Quintilian — time, place and persons present. However, an infinite number of details may be inquired into: such as the state of a room or a garden, the phases of the moon, the lamps which were lighted in a street, the food which was served at a meal, and all manner of things. Details of this kind may be relevant to break down an alibi, or to disprove an alleged conversation where only two persons were present: there is always some larger whole with which a

---

[54]   Cf. *The Trial of W. H. Wallace,* ed. W. F. Wyndham-Brown (Gollancz, 1933), pp. 139-140.

true story must dovetail, and development of an untrue story should disclose the points of discontinuity.

There are two ways in which collateral circumstances may be used. On the one hand, they may be used to lead the witness on to a point where he can be contradicted; on the other hand they may simply be used to enlarge the story until it is improbable or unbelievable or until it is apparent that the witness does not remember things which he would remember if his story was true.

(a) Leading the witness on

This is a frequent device. The object must be to lead the witness to state positive facts on which he can be contradicted by unquestionable evidence. This evidence may be part of one's own case, which the witness is deliberately led to contradict: alternatively it may be a fact of nature which can easily be verified, such as the fact that there was no moon on a certain night, or that gooseberries do not appear on the bushes in a certain month. Here is a self-explanatory example:[55]

'I understand you to say you saw the testator sign this instrument?' — 'I did .'

'And did you sign it at his request, as subscribing witness?' — 'I did.'

'Was it sealed with red or black wax?' — 'With red wax.'

'Did you see him seal it with red wax?' — 'I did.'

'Where was the testator when he signed and sealed his will?' — 'In his bed.'

'Pray, how long a piece of red wax did he use?' — 'About three inches long.'

'And who gave the testator this piece of wax?' — 'I did.'

'Where did you get?' — 'From the drawer of his desk.'

'How did he melt that piece of wax?' — 'With a candle.'

'Where did the candle come from?' — 'I got it out of a cupboard in the room.'

[55]   Quoted from Wellmann, *op. cit.*, pp. 159-160.

'How long should you say the candle was?' — 'Perhaps four or five inches long.'

'Do you remember who lit the candle?' — 'I lit it.'

'What did you light it with?' — 'Why, with a match.'

'Where did you get the match?' — 'On the mantel-shelf in the room.'

'Now, sir, upon your solemn oath, you saw the testator sign this will — he signed it in his bed — at his request you signed it as a subscribing witness — you saw him seal it — it was with red wax he sealed it — a piece of wax about three inches long — he lit the wax with a piece of candle which you procured from a cupboard — you lit the candle with a match which you found on a mantel-shelf?' — 'I did.'

'Once more, sir — upon your solemn oath, you did?' — 'I did.'

Counsel. 'My lord, you will observe this will is sealed with a wafer!'

In this case counsel has been careful to lead the witness to such a circumstantial story that it is quite evident on his being contradicted that he has made no honest mistake. It is no use conducting cross-examination of this sort without inducing the witness to express himself in the most deliberate and positive manner.

Alternatively, two witnesses, called by the other side may be led to contradict *one another* with regard to collateral facts which they must have observed, if their story is true. There is a celebrated example of this in the tale of Susanna and the Elders, in the thirteenth chapter of the Book of Daniel.[56] Two old men accused Susanna of adultery with a young man in a garden: they were questioned separately by Daniel, and when they were asked what sort of tree it was in the garden under which the adultery had taken place, one of them said that it was a holm tree, and the other said that it was a mastick tree.

---

[56]   In the post-Reformation Bibles this story appears separately in the Apocrypha.

(This, it seems, was in Babylonia, where trees are rare enough to be conspicious.)

(b) Showing improbability or lack of knowledge

In this procedure the object is not to bring out a contradiction, but to show that the witness does not remember circumstances which he ought to remember, and so to show that his story is untrue. In the Crippen case (pp. 79-80, *ante*), Crippen explained his suspicious conduct on board ship, before his arrest, as being the result of a conversation with a quartermaster. Sir Richard Muir cross-examined as follows to show that this conversation was imaginary:[57]

'What was his name?' — 'I do not know his name . . .'

'How many quartermasters were there?' — 'I believe there were four . . .'

'What was this one like?' — 'He was a little taller than I am, very thick-set, dark . . .'

'Any hair on his face?' — 'Yes, he had a moustache.'

'Is that all?' — 'That is all.'

'Had any of the other quartermasters got moustaches?' — 'Yes.'

'All of them?' — 'I am not sure.'[58]

'All dark?'—'I cannot say. I particularly noticed him. . .'

'Were all the quartermasters dark?' — 'I could not say.'

'All thick-set?' — 'No, some of them were tall and some of them were short.'

'Was this man the tallest or the shortest of them?' — 'He was of medium size.'

'Were any of the others medium?' — 'I think there was another medium size man.'

---

[57]   *Op. cit.,* p. 117.

[58]   Times change. A moustache would now be more conspicuous than it was in Edwardian days, just as a tree is more conspicuous in Mesopotamia than it is here.

'You would have no difficulty in distinguishing the man?' — 'Not if I saw him.'

Muir then turns to probing consequences:

'Did you ask your solicitor to find this quartermaster?' — 'No. I did not.'

'So far as you know, has any effort been made to bring that quartermaster here?' — 'No, not so far as I know.'

Rapid fire of questions

A special variety of this last-mentioned technique consists of a rapid fire of questions about details which a genuine witness would remember, but an untruthful witness would have to invent. The aim is to fire questions more swiftly than the witness can invent answers. There is a very fine example in the trial of Parrott, a former warrant officer of the Royal Navy, who was charged with spying and transmitting secret information to the Germans. The evidence showed that he had gone to Ostend and there had met a man who was a known German agent. Parrott's explanation was that a lady had arranged to meet him there, but to his surprise, the man turned up instead. The trial took place in 1913, and Sir John Simon (later Viscount Simon), who was then Solicitor-General, conducted the following cross-examination.[59] His purpose was to show that the lady was a product of Parrott's imagination.

'I should gather from what you say, that within a quarter of an hour, or twenty minutes, of the boat arriving you had learned that the lady was not coming?' — 'That is correct.'

'And that would be before nine o'clock?' — 'No. We did not sit down by the Inspector's witness until nine.'

'I thought it was as soon as you sat down that you asked where the lady was and were told?' — 'Exactly.'

'Then at nine o'clock you understood that the lady was not going to appear?' — 'Exactly.'

---

[59]   Quoted by Cassels, J. in his lecture on *Advocacy,* pp. 19-20.

'And there was nothing more to talk to Richard about?'
— 'There was a conversation ensued.'

'What about?' — 'He asked me how I came to make her acquaintance, and lots of other things which I have already mentioned.'

'Did you ask him anything?' — 'Yes, I asked him if he was any relative of hers, and he replied: "No"'

'Did you ask him who she was?' — 'No.'

'Did you ask him whether she was married?' — 'No.'

'Did you ask him what her occupation was?' — 'No.'

'Did you ask him whether she had got any lovers?' — 'No.'

'Did you ask him whether she was still travelling abroad?' — 'No.'

'Did you ask him whether she had left the lady companion she had spoken of?' — 'No.'

'Whether she was now in Switzerland?' — 'No.'

'Whether she was now in Germany?' — 'No.'

'Did you ask him why she had not come?'— 'No, I did not think to ask him that question.'

'Did you ask him whether she had got your telegram?' — 'No.'

'Did you ask him whether she had sent you a message?' — 'No.'

'Did you ask him how soon you could see her again?' — 'No.'

'Did you ask him where she could write to you?' — 'No.'

5 The technique of insinuation

The technique of insinuation consists of leading or forcing the witness, by adding facts at one point and modifying details at another, to give a version of his evidence which is more favourable to the other side. Its effect is, therefore, at one and the same time, to elicit favourable evidence and to weaken the evidence-in-chief. If this technique is skilfully employed, its effect is to give the story a totally new orientation, without altering the fundamental facts. It may also be used purely to elicit new and helpful evidence on topics which have not been covered in the examination-in-chief. There are two main forms of the technique: *gentle* insinuation, which is used with an impartial witness, or may be used with any sort of witness if the drift of the questions is concealed: and *firm* insinuation, which is used if the witness is hostile. Firm insinuation nearly always needs the support of strong material, whereas gentle insinuation can be conducted with or without material. In both forms there is usually a gradual approach, step by step, towards the important admissions, and this gradual style is characteristic of the technique; but in one form the witness is led, while in the other form he is driven.

This technique is highly flexible, and at the present day it is perhaps more popular than any other. It is significant that two of the most distinguished of modern cross-examiners — Sir Norman Birkett and Sir Roland Oliver — were particularly skilful at insinuation, while the two cross-examiners who were most accomplished in the use of probing (Hawkins) and confrontation (Carson) belonged to an earlier generation.[60] (This, of course, is a personal opinion with which others might not agree.)

---

[60]   Sir Patrick Hastings had a characteristic method of his own, which appears in nearly all his cases, e.g. in the cross-examinations of Prof. Laski and of Bob Sievier (*Cases in Court*, 1949, pp. 45-50, 61-69). At the outset he put quite plainly the essential points he intended to establish: these might be denied, but at all events the jury saw what was in issue. This was followed up by firm insinuation of detailed facts tending to prove the points, with ruthless surmounting of evasion. Finally, an admission of the essential points was forced, if possible. (Sir John Simon sometimes followed the same method, and perhaps both inherited it from Carson.) Hastings also quotes (*ibid.,* pp. 6-13) a most effective example of confrontation; and in cross-examining Lord Plender in the Royal Mail case (*ibid.,* pp. 223-225), he employed most

Insinuation has, besides, a special role in the conduct and tactics of a case which is denied to the other techniques. Even though the witness refuses to admit many of the points which are put to him, nevertheless the presentation of another version of the case, side by side with that elicited by the examination-in-chief, shows that there is something to be said on the other side. This constant foreshadowing, or reminder, of the evidence to be produced, or already produced, by the cross-examining advocate, is of great weight in cases tried by a jury.

(i) The scope of insinuation: some illustrations

The following examples illustrate — not, it is to be understood, exhaustively — the sort of points that may be brought out by insinuation.

(a) The limits of the evidence-in-chief

If the witness, in his evidence-in-chief, has failed to speak to an important point, it is useful to make this clear to the court: for instance, as in this extract from *The Trial of Dickman*.[61]

> *Mitchell-Innes,* K.C. 'You had an opportunity of identifying this man . . .?' — 'I had.'
> 'And you could not?' — 'I could not.'

(Another example from the same case is quoted on p.122, *post,* as it also illustrates the use of re-examination.)

(b) Explanatory facts

Where damaging facts have been proved in chief, an explanation may be obtained which weakens the damaging

---

skilfully the technique (unusual for him) of gentle insinuation.

[61] Ed. S. O. Rowan-Hamilton (1914), p. 56

inference. In *The Trial of Ley and Smith*[62] Minden, the hall
porter at a London hotel, deposed that Ley had paid him a
sum of money, the contention being that this was a reward
for the introduction of a man to assist Ley in an enterprise
of doubtful legality (actually to abduct the man who was
afterwards murdered). Sir Walter Monckton, K.C., cross-
examined as follows. (He was aware that Ley's wife had
previously stayed at the hotel in question.)

> 'At the time this money was given you, was the
> conversation a conversation in which he was saying that
> his wife was not coming back?' — 'Yes, that is what he
> said.'
>
> 'And it was his wife whom you had known well in the
> past as a resident in the hotel?' — 'Yes.'
>
> 'Ley himself you had known by sight?' — 'By sight for
> about four years, every day.'
>
> 'But I gather you had not had conversations with him?'
> — 'No.'
>
> 'When she was not there did he come to see about her
> letters and cables?' — 'Yes.'
>
> 'And you saw him from time to time?' — 'I saw him twice
> actually before he spoke to me.'
>
> 'I suppose Mrs. Ley was a person with whom you were
> quite well acquainted?' — 'Yes.'
>
> 'And it would not be an astonishing thing to you if she
> should, through Mr. Ley, make a present to you?' — 'That is
> what I rather expected.'
>
> 'Especially as she was not coming back again?' — 'May
> I elaborate that? I had sent two trunks of hers off to
> Australia, and I used to pay her newspaper bills and one or
> two things, and she said she would come back and see me on
> a certain day; but unfortunately she could not get back and
> went without seeing me.'

Observe that, without challenging the basic facts of the
incident, Sir Walter Monckton had caused a complete shift
in its interpretation: to alter the *interpretation* of awkward
facts is a most important objective in insinuation.

---

[62]   *Op. cit.*, pp. 67-68.

(c) Weakening an inference: suggesting other possibilities

In the Arran case (p. 77, *ante*), Duncan Coll said that the boots of the deceased had iron heels, which would be safer for climbing than ordinary boots: the inference being that an accidental slip over a cliff was unlikely. The Dean of Faculty said:

'I suppose that would depend very much on whether the metal was worn?' — 'It would.'

'If the metal was much worn, might not the iron both of the heels and of the springs become a source of danger instead of safety to a person going over smooth granite?' — 'Well, they might be slippery.'

In general, the force of circumstantial evidence depends on raising a probability. The mechanism of this kind of questioning is *to suggest other possibilities, equally consistent with the facts:* and this automatically weakens the probable inference. This form of examination (together with probing into the grounds of belief) is the main method of shaking expert opinion, and in this connection it is illustrated by the cross-examination of Dr. Fullarton in the Arran case, quoted at p. 78, *ante.*

(d) Other helpful facts

The next example, also from the Arran case,[63] shows the Dean of Faculty establishing points which will help his case generally: namely, the possibility of an accidental fall, as distinct from murder.

'You know the place where the body and the different things were found. Is it not a very rough place there?' — 'It is very rough . . . ; but some of the stones are smooth and polished.'

'Is it not a place where a person going down might slip?' — 'They generally pick their way.'

[63] *Op. cit.,* pp 89-90.

'But if they did not pick their way, and if a man made a mistake, might he not very readily slip?' — 'He might.'

'And are there not parts where, if a man were to slip, he would be very apt to pitch down heavily on his head?' — 'Yes, there are some precipices.'

'Is it not the case that if a man slipped, just about the place where the cap was found, he might go head-foremost over a drop of 30 feet?' — 'He might go a good length.'

'Would it not be quite enough to be damaging to the head?' — 'Yes.'

'Have you any doubt that if a man fell over there he would be killed?' — 'I do not know.'

The persistence shown by the Dean of Faculty in circumventing the successive hesitations of the witness in this passage is worth studying from a technical point of view.

(e) Possibility of mistaken observation.

With a firm knowledge of the fallacies of testimony, the suggestion can often be made to a witness that he is mistaken in his version of what he has seen or heard. This applies with particular force to the spoken word. In *The Trial of Ruxton,*[64] Dr. Ruxton was charged with murdering his wife and cutting up her body. One small point in the prosecution evidence was a cut on the doctor's hand, which he explained as having being caused in opening a tin of fruit. A Mrs. Hindson had knocked at the door on the morning in question, and she said in chief:

'The doctor . . . told me . . . that he had jammed his hand' —

the inference being that he had not had time to think out a convincing explanation for a cut caused by a surgical instrument in dissecting the body, and meant to convey that he had 'jammed' the hand in a door. Sir Norman Birkett asked in cross-examination:

---

[64]   Ed. Blundell and Wilson (1937), p. 43.

'Do you not think that he said "jabbed" and not
"jammed" when he spoke of his hand?' — 'No.'
Though the witness denied the suggestion, its effect would
not be lost on the jury.

In the trial of Ley and Smith, the defendant Smith said
that he understood from Ley (who had hired him to abduct
the murdered man) that the man had been dropped — safe
and sound, it was implied — at 'Wimbledon'. It so
happened that the dead body was found at a place called
'Woldingham': and prosecuting counsel, with grim irony,
asked Smith whether he was sure that Ley had not said
'Woldingham'.

Interpretation

Interpretation is just as important in evidence as actual
observation and the possibility of a mistaken interpretation
may in like manner be suggested. In the trial of a man
named Dacey for murder, the prisoner's mother, in support
of a plea of insanity, gave evidence that the prisoner had
always been peculiar, and mentioned some incidents in
point Hylton-Foster, K.C., asked whether these incidents
could not be explained on the basis that the prisoner lost
his temper if he did not get his way: to which the witness
agreed.

(ii) Gentle insinuation

First, to introduce this technique in a sustained form, an
extract is given from *The Trial of Roger Casement*[65] to
show its typical effect of altering the colour and atmosphere
of a story. Roger Casement was prosecuted for treason, the
substance of the charge being that he had gone round
prisoner-of-war camps in Germany to recruit Irish prisoners
to fight for the Germans in an Irish brigade. The witness
John Neill gave evidence to this effect: Sjt. Sullivan cross-

[65]   *Op. cit.,* p. 42.

examined him to show that the Irish Brigade was to fight on Irish soil only, at the end of the war, to defend Southern Ireland against the Ulster Volunteers. We are not concerned with the question whether this really helped the prisoner in point of law.

'Now, let us see what happened and the assurances given you in his speech that you did hear. You heard him say he was the organiser of the Irish Volunteers,[66] did not you?' — 'Yes.'

'That he was raising an Irish Brigade?' — 'Yes.'

'Was it in connection with the Irish Volunteers?' — 'Yes.'

'Did you hear him say that it had been subscribed for by Irish-Americans in America?' — 'Yes.'

'And that they were to fight in Ireland?' — 'Yes.'

'To win Home Rule?' — 'Yes.'

'Did he say fight in Ireland only?' — 'At that time only to fight in Ireland.'

'That was the basis on which they were being recruited?' — 'Yes.'

'Did he say that the war was nearly over?' — 'No: he never mentioned anything about the war being nearly over.'

'Did he speak of what might happen when the war was over?' — 'Yes.'

'When the war was over, if Germany won, did he say that the Irish Brigade could easily be landed in Ireland?' — 'Yes.'

'Did he say if Germany lost the war, on the other hand, they should go to America?' — 'Yes.'

'So if Germany won they were to go to Ireland?' — 'Yes.'

'And if they lost they were to go to America?' — 'Yes.'

The characteristic method of insinuation is to approach the critical questions with great caution, little by little, advancing by slow degrees and feeling one's way all the time. Thus, by the time the critical questions are reached, a foundation has been laid for them: moreover, the cross-examiner has some conception of what the answer will be, and there is less danger that a damaging reply will be given

[66]   A body formed in Ireland before the war.

unexpectedly. In other words, this is the way to approach the so-called 'dangerous question' which beginners are warned to avoid. Besides, one result of approaching by degrees the admissions desired is this, that if only a small point is asked each time, an adverse witness may not see the drift of the questions: to conceal the line of attack is always a good thing. The next two extracts illustrate the outstanding skill of Sir Roland Oliver in this sort of cross-examination. Both are taken from the trial of Wallace.[67] In this case Wallace was charged with the murder of his wife in her home. Now on the night in question he was out of the house for all but a fraction of the time when the murder could have been committed: in fact, he was looking for a bogus address to which he had been asked to go by a telephone message left at his chess club on the previous night, shortly before he arrived. The contention of the prosecution was that Wallace himself had sent this telephone call, to create a false alibi for himself. This is how Sir Roland Oliver questioned Mr. Beattie, the secretary of the chess club, who received the message:

'The part I am interested in particularly is the part in which the voice told you about the business, what it was. Can you remember what the voice said about that?' — 'Yes, I told him that Mr. Wallace was coming to the club that night, and he would be there shortly, would he ring up again. He said, "No, I am too busy; I have got my girl's 21st birthday on and I want to see Mr. Wallace on a matter of business; it is something in the nature of his business . . ." '

'In addition to that conversation, I suppose he spelt for you the name "Qualtrough"?' — 'Yes, at my request.'

'And gave the address?' — 'Yes.'

'And you had altogether quite a conversation with the voice?' — 'Yes, I should say so.'

[67] *The Trial of W. H. Wallace,* ed. W. F. Wyndham-Brown (1933) at pp. 89-90, 93-94; a case of outstanding technical and general interest, like the Arran murder.

'You used an expression in your evidence at the police court about the voice which you have not used today. You said a strong and gruff voice today.' — 'Yes.'

'At the police court you said it was a confident and strong voice?' — 'That means it was not a hesitating voice, in answer to some question.'

'So far as you could judge, was it a natural voice?' — 'That is difficult to judge.'

'. . . but did it occur to you that it was not a natural voice at the time?' — 'No, I had no reason for thinking that.'

'Do you know Mr. Wallace's voice well?' — 'Yes.'

'Did it occur to you that it was anything like his voice?' — 'Certainly not.'

'Does it occur to you now that it was anything like his voice?' — 'It would be a great stretch of imagination for me to say it was anything like that.'

Now a further factor in this case was that no one could suggest any reason why Wallace should kill his wife. He was a man of good character and was not known to have quarrelled with her. However, the latter point required very careful approach, as the slightest indication of any quarrel would have been damaging: in other words, to ask directly would have been a 'dangerous question'. The second extract shows the cautious approach to this matter. The witness here is Mr. Caird.

'You have known him for fifteen years?' — 'Yes.'

'What sort of a man is he as known to you?' — 'Well, a man who is intellectual, and varied in his habits of study, and that sort of thing.'

'With regard to his behaviour, is he a violent person or what?' — 'Oh, no, not at all, a placid man.'

'Have you ever seen any signs of a violent temper about him, or anything like that?' — 'Nothing whatever.'

'Would it be right to describe him as a studious man?' — 'Yes.'

'You knew his wife, did you not?' — 'Yes.'

'And family?' — 'Yes.'

'Are his habits known to you scientifically?' — 'Yes.'

'He has some kind of laboratory fixed up in his house?' — 'Yes in the back room he has a chemical laboratory.'

'Do you know that at one time or another he was giving lectures?' __ 'Yes, in the technical school in Byrom Street.'

'And playing a violin?' — 'Yes, he was only a beginner at that.'

'And chess?" — 'Yes . . .'

'How long had you known his wife?' — 'Well, not quite that long.'

'But a good many years?' — 'Yes . . .'

'Have you seen them often together?' — 'Yes, I have met them many a time. I used to see them in the park and in the street.'

'Would it be right to say, so far as you know, that they were generally together when he was not at work?' — 'Oh, yes.'

'So far as their relations were concerned, were they happy?' — 'Yes.'

'So far as you could observe?' — 'So far as I could see.'

'You have never seen anything to the contrary?' — 'Nothing whatever.'

'At any rate, you visited him, and that was as recent as last year?' — 'Yes.'

'Were their relations still just the same?' — 'Yes, quite good.'

'Would it be fair to suggest that from your observation they were a devoted couple?' — 'Yes.'

'Would that be putting it too high? Use your own phrase.' — 'Well, I should say they were a happy couple, a very happy couple.'

A gradual approach like this has a starting-point (the *terminus a quo*) and a conclusion (the *terminus ad quem*). The *terminus ad quem,* of course, is the material point to be extracted from the witness, which is visualised as the objective from the start. The *terminus a quo* will be something which is common ground — either something said in chief, or some other point which will not be disputed. Then it is just a matter of passing by stages from one to the other, like an acrostic in a newspaper: but an

accomplished advocate like Sir Roland Oliver does not need
to work out the stages in advance, he does it as a matter of
skilled habit. However, an inexperienced advocate might
well find it a useful exercise to work out questions leading
by degrees from one point to another, concealing the
objective so far as possible.

(iii) Firm insinuation

Firm insinuation and gentle insinuation shade into one
another, according to the resistance of the witness and the
material available to support the suggestions.
Nevertheless, firm insinuation has marked characteristics of
its own. Instead of admissions being extracted gently, they
are *forced*, and the witness is driven on by the remorseless
pressure of facts. Therefore, facts must be available to
support the questions: the cross-examiner must be ready to
use confrontation to destroy the witness's denials. It is
noticeable that defendants tend to use gentle insinuation —
because they have not yet called their witness — while
plaintiffs and prosecutors tend to use the firm technique,
which is especially prominent in cross-examining the
prisioner in a criminal case. Like gentle insinuation, firm
insinuation proceeds step by step, but not so much for
reasons of caution: the object is more to force admissions
point by point, so that they may receive full weight. In
The Trial of Crippen[68] one of the main pieces of evidence
against the doctor was the fact that he had taken to flight.
Sir Richard Muir cross-examined him on the following
lines:

> 'You thought you were in danger of arrest?' — 'Yes.'
> 'And so you fled the country?' — 'Yes.'
> 'Under a false name?' — 'Yes.'
> 'Shaved off your moustache?' — 'Yes.'

[68]   Ed. Filson Young (1920), p. 112. Miss Le Neve was the
woman the doctor was in love with, for whose sake he
murdered his wife.

'Left off wearing your glasses in public?' — 'Yes.'
'Took Le Neve with you?' — 'Yes.'
'Under a false name?' — 'Yes.'
'Posing as your son?' — 'Yes.'
'Went to Antwerp?' — 'Yes.'
'Stayed in an hotel there?' — 'Yes.'

In this example the facts in question had already been proved by the prosecution and were indisputable. The next example is taken from *The Trial of Dickman*.[69] Dickman was charged with murdering a man on a train, in order to steal money which was being taken to a colliery for the payment of wages. Tindal Atkinson, K.C., in cross-examining the prisoner to strengthen his case by showing knowledge and opportunity, had to surmount a good deal of evasion.

'You say you know the deceased man?' — 'I knew the deceased man; but if I had been asked off-hand what his name was, I could not have told you.'

'Did you not know his name?' — 'No, if any one had said to me "Do you know Nisbet?" after a description, I would have know the man.'

'I do not understand you. Did you know his name, or did you not?' — 'Yes, but if I had been asked off-hand, I would not be able to call the man Nisbet.'

'But you knew his name was Nisbet?' — 'Yes.'

'Did you know this man by name?' — 'Yes, I did know him by name.'

'On the 18th March did you know this man by name?' — 'I did.'

'Did you know what he was?' — 'I knew he was a clerk on the quay . . .'

'Did you know he was clerk and book-keeper to a colliery company?' — 'No I did not . . .'

'You have been connected with a colliery?' — 'Yes.'

'Do you know that wages are paid once a fortnight?' — 'I do.'

69   *Op. cit.*, pp. 113-115.

'Do you know they are usually paid on a Friday?' — 'Yes.'

'Do you know that wages are usually taken from . . . Newcastle to the collieries?' — 'No, I could not say that — in fact, to any particular colliery.'

'Money has to be drawn from the bank?' — 'Yes . . .'

'And carried by some one?' — 'Yes.'

'To the colliery where wages had to be paid?' - 'Yes.'

'You knew that?' — 'Yes, I had done the same business myself . . .'

'I suppose you know they are usually carried in a bag of some sort?' — 'Yes.'

'A leather bag?' — 'I could not say . . . but cash bags are usually leather.'

The last quotation under this heading is taken from the libel action, *Cadbury v. Daily News.*[70] The newspaper had accused Mr. W. A. Cadbury of making profits out of cocoa grown on a Portuguese island by slave labour (the truth being that, on becoming aware of the situation, he tolerated it for a while in the hope, which proved to be vain, of bringing about improvements).   Carson's cross-examination of Cadbury gave deadly weight to every detail:

'Is it a fact that San Thome cocoa has been slave grown to your knowledge for eight years? — 'Yes.'

'Was it slavery of a very atrocious character?' — 'Yes.'

'The cocoa you were buying was procured by atrocious methods of slavery?' — 'Yes.'

'Men, women and children taken forcibly from their homes against their will?' — 'Yes.'

'Were they marched like cattle?' — 'I cannot answer that question. They were marched in forced marches down to the coast.'

'Were they labelled when they went on board the ship?' — 'Yes.'

'How far had they to march? — 'Various distances. Some came from more than a thousand miles, some from quite near the coast.'

[70]   E. Marjoribanks, *Life of Lord Carson*, Vol. 1 (1932), pp. 395-397.

'Never to return again?' — 'Never to return.'

'. . . did they go down in shackles?' — 'It is the usual custom to shackle them at night on the march.'

'Those who could not keep up with the march were murdered?' — 'I have seen statements to that effect . . .'

'The men, women and children are freely bought and sold?' — 'I did not believe . . . that there has been anything that corresponded to the open slave-market of fifty years ago. It is done now more by subtle trickery . . .'

'You do not suggest that it is better because done by subtle trickery?' — 'No.'

'The children born to the women . . . become the property of the owners of the slaves?' — 'I believe that children born on the estates do.'

'Was it not the most cruel and atrocious form of slavery that ever existed?' — 'I cannot distinguish between slavery and slavery. All slavery is atrocious.'

'Knowing it was atrocious, you took the main portion of your supply of cocoa for the profit of your business from the islands conducted under this system?' — 'Yes, for a period of some years.'

In conclusion, Carson asked one of those telling questions which finish off a cross-examination with real artistry:

'Have you formed any estimation of the number of slaves who lost their lives in preparing your cocoa during those eight years?' — 'No, no, no.'

If a witness is unlikely to answer a question if put to him in general terms, it is a good method — much used in firm insinuation — to put detailed examples in proof of the general proposition. An example is given on p. 108, *post,* where Sir John Simon, to force an admission that a woman lived expensively, asked detailed questions about clothing, jewellery and expensive hotels.

(iv) Insinuation to elicit fresh evidence

This calls for no special comment, except that it opens up a new aspect of the case not covered by the evidence-in-chief: the method followed, as a rule, will be the cautious approach as in gentle insinuation. Below is an extract from *The Trial of Ley and Smith*,[71] where Sir Walter Monckton, K.C., uses Ley's housekeeper — called by the prosecution — to help to construct an alibi for Ley, i.e. to show that he was away from his house at the time the murder took place there.

'Did you post a letter . . .?' — 'Yes.'

'Then what did you do?' — 'I turned from the letter box and I saw Mr. Ley passing under the lamp standard.'

'Which way was he going?' — 'He was going towards Brompton Road.'

'Had he a hat and coat on?' — 'Yes.'

(By the Lord Chief Justice). 'What time was this?' — 'This would be about a quarter past five, as far as I can remember.'

'. . . Did you come out again?' — 'I came out from No. 8 about twenty past six.'

'Did you come past No. 5?' — 'I passed No. 5.'

'Did you see any signs of life from any floor or window?' — 'There was no sign of life or light in the place.'

(v) Insinuating converging lines of fact

It is frequent practice to insinuate converging lines of fact which, taken together, lead to a probable conclusion: such as facts showing opportunity and motive for a crime. The cross-examination of a prisoner often starts with some general questions on these lines: though there may be no admissions, the effect of the questions and the prisoner's reactions are noticed by the jury. On the trial of Vera Boulton[72] for poisoning her child, the main evidence was that after she visited the boy in hospital he fell into a coma, and that she was seen to give him something which tasted nasty, also a drink and some sweets. Paley Scott, K.C., cross-examined as follows:

---

[71]   *Op. cit.*, p. 125.
[72]   Leeds Assizes, December, 1944.

'Do I understand that Colin was always rather a sickly child?' — 'Yes sir.'

'And suffered a great deal?' — 'Yes.'

'Did you think perhaps that it would be better for him if he were dead?' — 'No.'

So far, *motive* is suggested.

'Have you ever had to give either of your children a doctor's pill?' — 'I can't remember, no.'

'Have you ever had to take one yourself?' — 'Well, just Aspro or anything . . .'

'And it is easier to take aspirin, or any other tablet, is it not, if you drink something to help to wash it down?' — 'Yes, sir.'

'Have you ever given either of your children medicine that the doctor has sent?' — 'Yes, sir.'

'Sometimes, I suppose, they have not liked it?' — 'Well, no, sir.'

'And do you say, when you are going to give them medicine: If you take this like a good little boy . . . I will give you a sweet?' — 'Yes, I may have done.'

These questions brought out the probable *method.*

So, in quite a short space, the essence of the whole case was put to the witness and to the jury. There is a more complex example — too long to quote — in Sir John Simon's cross-examination of Mr. Robinson in *The Mr. 'A' Case.*[73] Sir John established in turn that (1) Mr. Robinson's wife was pretty (2) she lived expensively (3) Robinson had no money of his own (4) he received money from his wife (5) she received men in her flat — thus paving the way for the inference that Robinson lived by means of his wife's activities and contacts with other men.

6 The technique of undermining

Undermining, or cross-examination as to credit, is a most important technique and deserves a lengthy treatment.

[73]   Ed. C. E. Bechhofer Roberts.

Unfortunately, it is hard to find examples suitable for quotation: but at all events the principles can be indicated.

Undermining is not really a separate technique: it is the use of the other techniques for a new objective, not to cross-examine on the facts but to show that the witness cannot be relied on to tell an accurate or truthful story. Its aim is to cut away the foundations of the evidence. At its best it is swift, short and decisive, but only too often cross-examination to credit is long-winded and inconclusive.

Broadly, the object is to show that either (i) the witness does not really know what he is talking about, or (ii) though he may know the truth, he is not telling it. The sub-headings which follow may not be exhaustive.

(i) No sufficient opportunity to observe

To prove that there was no sufficient opportunity to observe strikes away the foundations of valid observation. There are all sorts of possibilities, some of which have been discussed in the section on the fallacies of observation (p. 19, *ante*). The witness — having mistaken the date — may not have been on the scene at all at the time he states. If there, he may have been too far away to see, or the light may have been bad. He may have been too far away to hear properly, or a great deal of noise may have been going on. All such facts can be brought out by probing and insinuation.

Another important question is whether the witness was giving his attention to the facts he reports — whether, e.g. he was watching the traffic at all before he heard a loud crash, or was giving his attention to the whole of a long conversation. In *The Laski Libel Action,*[74] the main issue was whether Prof. Laski, arguing with a heckler from an

[74]   Verbatim Report (Daily Express, 1947), pp. 135-137.

election platform, had used words 'openly advocating revolution', which the professor denied. A distinguished air force officer, the Parliamentary candidate, who was sitting beside Laski, said that he had been listening but no such words were used. Sir Patrick Hastings, K.C., swiftly asked the witness whether he had heard certain other words — which undoubtedly had been used — and the witness said that he had not. This clearly showed that the witness had not heard everything, and so undermined his evidence.

'Do you recognise this expression: "It does not lie in the mouth of any member of the Tory Party, who helped to organise a mutiny in the British Army over Home Rule in 1914, to discuss the question of violence"? Do you remember anything like that being said by anybody?' — 'No, I do not. That does not mean it wasn't said.'

'Many things may have been said which you did not hear?' — 'There was nothing vital that I would not have heard.'

'If you did not hear it, how do you know whether it was vital or not?'

In the Arran case[75] a witness named Cosimo Latona stated that he was a 'guide' in the Arran mountains and that the place where the body was found was a dangerous one: this was to support the defence theory that the dead man might have slipped accidentally. Graham Murray (Viscount Dunedin) asked these questions:

'How long have you been in Arran?' — 'About three years.'

'Are you a fisherman by trade?' — 'Yes, a fisherman in the winter.'

'How many times have you guided people over the hills in Arran?' — 'I did not guide any people until the body of Rose was found.'

'Had you ever been in Glen Sannox at all before Rose's body was found?' — 'No.'

[75] *Op. cit.,* p. 169.

(ii) Attacking the qualifications of an expert

This is a dangerous procedure, and it is nearly always unwise to attack an expert's qualifications in connection with the particular topic on which he has come prepared to give evidence. The safest course is to search for a collateral matter, which the witness ought to know if he really is an expert. Sir Norman Birkett prosecuted in a murder case (the trial of Rouse) where part of the evidence concerned the remains of a burnt-out car, and an 'expert' came forward for the defence to draw very confident conclusions from the state of the remains. Sir Norman just put one question to him:

'What is the co-efficient of the expansion of brass?' — and the witness quite unable to answer, left the witness box in confusion.[76]

(iii) Bias

Facts showing bias may be elicited, but it is more convincing if the witness is encouraged to talk and led on to show his bias by exaggerated statements.

(iv) Previous inconsistent statements

These also may be elicited to attack the witness's credit, but it is much more impressive to use them as material for confrontation — i.e. to destroy the evidence given on the facts.

(v) Distortion by memory and imagination

When distortion by memory and imagination is suspected, the most effective way of exposing this to the court is to trace the growth of the distortion. If, for instance, two statements have been given on successive occasions, and there is a difference between the two, it may be useful to

[76] Bowker, *Behind the Bar,* p. 216.

trace any conversations which took place between the two dates, any discussions overheard, or reports in the press, or suggestive questions which have been put to the witness. When identification is in issue, it may be useful to inquire whether anyone was pointed out before an identification parade,[77] or whether his photograph appeared in the press. The difficulty is that one is usually working in the dark. This is no doubt the reason why effective cross-examination of this sort is rare, but it has big possibilities, and a little probing to detect influences making for distortion may yield unexpected results.

(vi) Facts showing dishonesty: previous convictions

Previous convictions do not, in themselves show that the witness is unworthy of belief. What is important is to elicit the facts of previous dishonest conduct in such a way that the court will see that the witness has no scruples about lying if it serves his purpose. The great advantage of a conviction is that the witness, if he is evasive, can at once be confronted with it, and the conviction can be proved. A witness can be cross-examined equally well about conduct which did *not* result in a conviction, but in this case his denials cannot be contradicted. The procedure, therefore, in a case where the witness has (e.g.) a previous conviction for false pretences might consist of a series of questions like this:

'Were you in Birmingham in 1928?'
'Did you know a Mr. Brown?'
'Did you obtain a cheque for £200 from him?'
'Did you cash it?'
'And was that cheque obtained by the false pretence that you had a motor car for sale?'
'It was untrue that you had a motor car, was it not?'

[77] There is some rather unimpressive cross-examination of this sort in *The Trial of Dickman*.

'Were you tried at the Assizes?'

'At your trial, did you swear that you had made no such statement?'

'Did the jury refuse to believe you?'

'Were you convicted?'

'And sent to prison for two years?'

'Were you telling the truth to the jury then?'

'And are you telling the truth now?'

Such an approach carries much more weight than simply asking the question: Have you been convicted of obtaining money by false pretences? — a question which will almost certainly bring forward the suggestion that there was a miscarriage of justice and that the witness is a greatly wronged man.

7 Subsidiary techniques

(i) Pinning down an evasive witness

It is always necessary to be able to pin down an evasive witness to precise admissions and denials. This may be done either for the purpose of ascertaining exactly what has to be destroyed — for instance, as a preliminary to confrontation — or for the purpose of leading on to further admissions. There is a good example in *The Laski Libel Action*.[78] In this case Prof. Laski sued a newspaper which published a report that he had 'openly advocated revolution' from an election platform. One of the defences was justification, based partly on the many books which the plaintiff had written for years and years. The professor stated in evidence (in effect) that he had not made the reported remarks: that he did indeed believe in 'revolution' in the sense of a 'social transformation'; that he thought if 'revolution' in this sense did not come by consent, it would come by violence; and that he himself was not in favour of violence, but was giving a warning that, in the absence of

[78]   *Op. cit.,* pp. 69-70

peaceful change, violence could not be stopped. As a preliminary to confronting the professor with passages from his books, Sir Patrick Hastings, K.C., cross-examined him as follows:

'Mr. Laski, do you believe that the use of violence to achieve your political ends is practically inevitable?' — 'No. In a country where there is a long constitutional tradition of mature and literate people, I think that consent —'

'Is the answer "no"?' — 'The answer is "no".'

'. . . Have you ever believed that which I have put to you?' — 'No.'

'Do you agree with me that anyone who for years had preached such a doctrine would be a public menace?' — 'No, not necessarily.'

'Have you ever preached it?' — 'No.'

'You do not think that such a person would be necessarily a public danger?' — 'I do not understand quite what you mean by that.'

'. . . Supposing a person for years was preaching this doctrine to a dissatisfied proletariat, "The use of violence to achieve your political aims is practically inevitable", do not you think such a person would be a public danger?' — 'That would depend upon the degree of his power to persuade those to whom he spoke.'

'Would you consider yourself . . . a person sufficiently powerful to be a public danger?' — 'I should have said not.'

'In this court you would say not. On public platforms you take rather a different view, do you not?' — [The answer in substance was, No.]

'In the circumstances . . . on the 11th June 1945 . . . did you then believe that if the aims of the proletariat could not be achieved without the use of violence, then violence was justifiable?' — 'No.'

'Do you agree that anyone who preached that doctrine would be a public danger?' — 'Yes.'

This point took a great deal of time to reach.

(ii) **Descending into detail**

It often happens that, if a question is put in a general form,
the witness is able to deny or evade it. If, on the other hand,
questions are put about particular facts which go to
establish the same general result, it is not so easy to deny
them. This method is used chiefly in connection with firm
insinuation, and, like 'pinning down', is useful in dealing
with an evasive witness. In *The Mr. 'A' Case*[78a] Sir John
Simon had to cross-examine Mr. Robinson, an extremely
slippery and evasive witness: he wanted to insinuate the fact
that Robinson's wife lived expensively, and this is how he
did it:

'Is she a lady who dresses expensively?' — 'Yes, I
should say so.'

'. . . I see cheques of Mrs. Robinson's to Paquin, to Gray,
to Redferns, to Revillons, and so on; so we may assume she
wore expensive clothes?' — 'It is fair to suggest so, yes.'

'She has some real pearls, hasn't she?' — 'She had.'

'And she has dealt from time to time quite extensively
with jewellers?' — 'Yes.'

'When she goes abroad, does she stay at the very best
hotels?' — 'I could not tell you that.'

'Let me suggest one or two: The Hotel de Paris at Monte
Carlo?' — 'I was not aware that she had stayed there.'

'Do you know the hotel?' — 'I know the hotel.'

'It's a pretty good hotel, is it not?' — 'A very good
hotel.'

'And in Paris at Claridge's Hotel?' — 'That I don't know
anything about.'

'In London at the Hotel Cecil?' — 'Yes, I am aware she
stayed there.'

(iii) **Dividing long questions into short, sharp questions**

This, again, is specially characteristic of firm insinuation:
see the admirable example from the Crippen case, at p. 96,

[78a] *Op. cit.*, p. 54.

ante. In gentle insinuation questions may similarly be short and simple though not sharp.

(iv) Rapid fire of questions

This is peculiar to probing: see p. 84, *ante.*

(v) Surprise

The use of surprise may be as effective in the tactics of litigation as in warfare. If there is a witness who must at all costs be broken down, it is an effective technique to take the witness by surprise and throw him off balance by the very first question. Perhaps the most famous example is the question put by Sir Rufus Isaacs K.C. (Lord Reading) to Seddon, who was accused of poisoning his lodger for her money:

> 'Did you like her?'

This was an attack from so unexpected a direction that Seddon did not know what to say.[79]

According to Mr. Bowker,[80] Sir Norman Birkett sometimes spent hours studying his first question in difficult cross-examinations.

However, a surprise does not need to be sprung at the start, but may be held up till later: see the example of the surprise question, 'Did you kiss him?', from the cross-examination of Wilde, quoted at p. 71, *ante.*

---

[79] *Trial of the Seddons,* ed. by F. Young (1914), p. 170. Actually it was the second question.

[80] *Behind the Bar,* p. 235.

Chapter 6

Cross-Examination: Preparation and Planning

1 Preparation

The preparation of the case is the responsibility of the solicitor, advised from time to time, as requisite, by junior counsel. In this task, the proofs of one's own witnesses are the chief elements, but the preparation of material for cross-examination ought not to be overlooked. If it is believed that a party or other witness on the opposite side is likely to tell a false story, or is badly mistaken, as much material as possible should be made available for use against him. The general character, prejudices and background of a hostile witness — or, indeed, of any witness who is likely to be called — are valuable facts for this purpose: and *documentary* evidence, which can be used to contradict or qualify his story, is of special value. These points should be remembered at the discovery stage, in examining documents disclosed by the other side or in searching for undisclosed documents. Interrogatories, likewise, can be useful material.

Once in a while, big cases occur where an action is brought or defended by a bold impostor who can probably be unmasked if sufficient material can be collected to shatter him: on such occasions, if the money at issue is considerable or the issues are of great consequence to the parties, it may be proper to employ inquiry agents. It is doubtful whether the defendants in the Oscar Wilde case or the Mr. 'A' case would have been successful — though they engaged the most distinguished advocates of their day — if their solicitors had not been alert enough to take this course. However, cases of this magnitude are few and far between.

2 Choice of technique

Confrontation, in its massive form, is not a technique which can be used every day. It is suitable, really, only for cases where a great mass of material has been collected, where the witness to be attacked is believed to have feet of clay, and the intention is to strike a knock-out blow. On the other hand, in its lesser form, confrontation with some specific unquestionable fact, it is in constant use. In probing, it is used to trap a witness who has been led on to elaborate the details of his story until they can be challenged: in gentle insinuation, it is used quietly to convince a witness that he has made an honest mistake: in firm insinuation it is used to surmount evasion and denials: finally, in undermining it is used for the same purpose, for example by confronting the witness with a certificate of a conviction which he has refused to admit, or with a previous contradictory statement.

Probing is also in constant use, but especially to show up the absurdity of a false story, or to trace the origin of a mistake. If, however, there is any doubt about the most suitable method to adopt, it is always best to choose insinuation: insinuation should, as a rule, start with the gentle approach (keeping the object concealed) until it is clear that firm pressure must be applied: and even then, material must be available for firm insinuation, if it is to be effective.

Where a story is partly true and partly false, probing and insinuation are used in close association, with swift transitions from one to the other. Thus the false parts of the story will be probed into, and immediately afterwards the true version will be insinuated: when the cross-examiner reaches the true parts of the story he will, as far as is necessary, use insinuation with these to give the facts a strong colouring in his own favour. This alternating method is very noticeable in the cross-examination of prisoners at criminal trials.[81] To illustrate the rapid alternation, here is a summary of the opening and closing part of the cross-examination of Dickman by E. Tindal Atkinson, K.C. (Dickman was charged with murdering a man on a railway train, to rob him of the wages he was carrying to a colliery.)

1. *Insinuates* that Dickman knew Nisbet well, also knew that he carried wages on Fridays. (See the extract quoted at p. 97, *ante*.)
2. *Probes* Dickman's journey to see Hogg a fortnight before and establishes that there was no good reason for it. (On the occasion of the murder Dickman said that he was travelling to see Hogg again: the prosecution contention was that he travelled to rob Nisbet and for no other purpose.)
3. *Insinuates* Dickman knew the wages were being taken on that train to Morpeth.

---

[81] See, e.g. the cross-examination of Wallace by E. G. Hemmerde, K.C., in *The Trial of Wallace*, pp. 190-221, which is in the characteristic style of criminal prosecutions; also the long cross-examination of Seddon by Rufus Isaacs, K.C. (Lord Reading) which is chiefly sustained firm insinuation and probing on matters of detail: *The Trial of the Seddons*, pp. 170-226.

4.   *Insinuates* Dickman met Nisbet at the station and accompanied him in the same carriage. *Confronts* him with the witnesses who saw them together and *probes* his answers (e.g. to show the absurdity of saying that Hepple, an old friend of Dickman's, could be mistaken in identifying him).

5.   *Probes* Dickman's story that he travelled at the back of the train, not with Nisbet at the front. *Probes* further by questioning him about the passengers in the carriage. *Confronts* him with the fact that Hepple was standing near the very compartment in which he says he travelled, but did not see him.

   [The intervening parts are not quoted as they would require detailed explanation of the evidence.]

12.   *Insinuates* that Dickman knew the abandoned pit shaft where the empty cash bag was found. Dickman denies this, and is *confronted* with the evidence of a mine official to the contrary effect.

13.   *Confronts* with bloodstained gloves and trouser pocket, and stain (not proved to be blood) on fawn coat. *Probes* explanations to show that they are unconvincing.

14.   *Probes* Dickman's statement that he had plenty of money. *Pins down* to October. *Confronts* with visit to moneylender in October. *Probes* explanation. *Confronts* with another loan, the pawning of jewellery, and the smallness of his bank account and other savings.

The whole of this cross-examination is worth studying as an example of skilful cross-examination.

Undermining should be employed, as a rule, only as a last resort, when there is no other way of getting over adverse evidence. It should not be done, of course, when it it desired to elicit positive evidence from the witness — unless, that is, the attempt fails.

3 Minor witnesses

In most cases, the majority of the witnesses play a very small part, testifying to little points which are pieced together to form a composite whole. Unless there is good reason for employing some other method, gentle insinuation should be used with these witnesses, to give a favourable colouring to their fragment of evidence and to extract small admissions which can be used to build up one's own case.

Where there is a piece of adverse evidence which cannot be toned down by insinuation, and there is no material with which the witness can be confronted, he should be challenged distinctly with the suggestion that he is mistaken. If there is any possibility of doing so, he should be undermined by a few swift, well-chosen questions, as in Sir Patrick Hastings' cross-examination quoted at p. 103, *ante*.

The questioning of these minor witnesses does not call for detailed preparation, beyond a general knowledge of the sort of tactics indicated.

4 Major witnesses

When there are real issues of fact, there is always at least one major witness — often the opposite party — who has to be cross-examined thoroughly, and there may be two or three others. The tactics to be used against such major witnesses — especially the plaintiff or defendant, the prisoner in a criminal trial, the husband or wife in matrimonial causes — need to be planned with great care.[82]

---

[82]   Sir Patrick Hastings seems to say (*Cases in Court,* pp. 334-335) that cross-examination ought not to be planned, but ought to be thought out with lightning rapidity at the conclusion of the evidence-in-chief, after measuring the psychological make-up of the witness and discerning the weak points. Not everybody can think so rapidly.

(i) The choice of technique

This is governed by the factors explained in section 2, p. 111, *ante*. Leaving aside the exceptional cases suitable for massive confrontation, it may be said broadly that there are three alternatives:

(a)   With a witness who is believed to be honest and impartial, a sustained use of gentle insinuation, changing to firm insinuation if unavoidable, but not otherwise;

(b)   With other witnesses, gentle insinuation as far as it seems likely to go; then a mixture of probing, firm insinuation and confrontation, as in the example quoted from the Dickman case (firm insinuation is here the *dominant* technique);

(c)   With a witness who cannot otherwise be shaken, sustained and deliberate undermining from the start, or from the point where (b) fails.

The actual choice is, of course, an exercise of practical judgment, for which no unvarying rules can be laid down.

(ii) The start

A form of opening tactics adopted quite frequently, even with a 'tough' witness, consists of gentle insinuation of a broad character on the general background of the case, for

---

Moreover, I find this view difficult to reconcile with Sir Patrick's own carefully planned questions to Prof. Laski and Lord Plender (*ibid.,* pp. 45-50, 223-225) and with the remark at p. 284: 'A line of cross-examination which sounds admirable in consultation may be totally destroyed by one unexpected answer, and so *every possible line of approach must be thoroughly explored*'. Is not the truth this? — that it is a mistake to work out a series of detailed questions word for word, but that the general line of attack should be planned, while remaining flexible and even liable to be discarded up to the very last minute.

instance, motive and opportunity to commit a crime: good illustrations are to be found in Paley Scott's opening questions to Vera Boulton (p. 101, *ante*.) and Tindal Atkinson's opening questions to Dickman (p. 97 *ante*.)

Another method — which can have striking results — is to plan a surprise question, which will take the witness off his balance right at the start. As shown on p. 109, *ante*, such distinguished advocates as Sir Rufus Issacs (the first Marquess of Reading) and Sir Norman Birkett took great trouble to plan their first question on these lines.[83-4]

(iii) The order

All good cross-examinations follow an orderly arrangement according to topics, varied by sudden returns to critical points with the object of taking the witness by surprise. Gentle insinuation and firm insinuation tend, in addition, to follow chronological order, or at any rate the same order as the evidence-in-chief: this has the advantage that important points will not be overlooked accidentally. Confrontation follows the order of *weight* — i.e. the most damaging facts are best reserved to the end, the smaller points being taken first.

(iv) The last question[83-4]

The ideal of every cross-examiner is to make his last question a Parthian shot. For an outstanding example, see Carson's last question to Mr. Cadbury (p. 99, *ante*).

[83-4] Sir Patrick Hastings likewise attached importance to the first and last questions (*op. cit.*, pp. 336-338). His first questions however, were not thought out carefully in advance, nor, as a rule, were they surprise questions: rather they took the form of a 'straight left' — a blunt question to show the witness that he was challenged.

5 Types of witnesses

It is not at all helpful to classify witnesses into types, because no two liars are alike, nor any two honestly mistaken witnesses. Such examples as 'the canting hypocrite' and 'the awkward witness', while pointing a limited moral, do not represent any firm classes of persons. A broad division may be made into those who are both truthful and accurate, those who are honestly mistaken, and those who are biased or lying. This does suggest different lines of approach, but should not be taken too rigidly. For experts, too, special considerations arise.

(i) Honest and accurate witnesses

Viscount Maugham says:[85]
> 'The art of cross-examining a witness of truth who is wholly disinterested and unafraid and is neither vain nor nervous is simply to ask questions the answers to which will not make the matter worse.'

This perhaps simplifies the matter too much: the technique of gentle insinuation should be applied both to bring out any favourable facts which have not been mentioned and to modify the general tone of the evidence.

(ii) Honestly mistaken witnesses

The whole of the section in Chapter 2 on the fallacies of testimony is relevant. The main sources of error are bad observation, bad interpretation, faulty memory, and imagination (all of them closely influenced by personal interest or bias, notably in divorce cases). The keys for disclosing the mistakes and establishing the truth are

---

[85]   *The Tichborne Case*, p. 303.

probing and insinuation.[86] It should not be overlooked that parties frequently bring and defend actions because they are honestly (but mistakenly) convinced that they are in the right.

(iii) Liars

Every one of the techniques may be appropriate, from confrontation to undermining: perhaps the most usual is a combined testing of the story by probing and (firm) insinuation. There are three familiar 'traps' for a lying witness:

(a)   Confronting him with something bit by bit, leading him to give false explanation, (before he knows all the facts) which will involve him in contradictions.

(b)   Probing so as to lead him to assert details which can be contradicted.

(c)   Gentle insinuation by distinct lines of thought, the object of which is concealed, and which converge to establish something which has been denied.

There are also some old devices for dealing with children, or uneducated witnesses, who have learnt their story by heart. These may be encouraged to repeat their story, and to add details about collateral circumstances; then to repeat it again, when their answers to the questions about details may be different. Alternatively, the witness may be confused by being asked to repeat his story out of order. Witnesses of this kind are seldom encountered nowadays, but occasions may arise when these devices can still be used.

---

86   For a brilliant example of probing and insinuation to show the genesis of a mistake in identification, see Carson's cross-examination of the postmistress in the Archer-Shee case (where a naval cadet was unjustly accused of stealing a postal order): Marjoribanks, *Life,* Vol. 1, pp. 423 et seq.

(iv) Experts[87]

An expert opinion consists of a conclusion, drawn from facts, which may or may not be true, by inferences, which may or may not be sound.

The first approach is therefore by the technique of probing, to elucidate precisely the facts and inferences on which the conclusion rests.

The next step is to suggest that if the facts are not quite as the expert has been led to believe, the conclusion will be different: in short, to use the technique of insinuation to establish other *possibilities*. (It is nearly always insinuation of possibilities, not facts, in dealing with experts.)

A third possible step is to challenge the validity of the inferences which have been drawn (assuming the facts as stated by the expert). This is again a form of insinuation of possibilities: but the cross-examiner is here on very delicate ground, and he must be ready to confront the expert with authoritative passages from books on medicine (or whatever subject it may be).

The final method of attacking an expert is to attack his qualifications — in short, to undermine his competence to form an opinion on the matter. Such an attack should not be directed to the subject on which the witness has prepared his evidence, but to something collateral, within the scope of his qualifications. An attempt to undermine an expert is always risky. It is encouraging to reflect, however, that few lawyers could stand an unexpected cross-examination on (shall we say) the law of restraint of trade, where their vague answers might be confronted with the authoritative speeches of Lord Macnaghten: some of the stories about the discrediting of medical and other experts suggest that their

---

[87] See further pp. 71, 104, *ante*. For a skilful cross-examination of a medical expert, see Marshall Hall's cross-examination of Dr. Willcox in *The Trial of the Seddons,* ed. F. Young (1914), pp. 112-130.

general knowledge of their subject is often as vague as our own.

Chapter 7

Re-Examination

1 General

The object of re-examination is to explain or qualify admissions made by the witness when cross-examined: that is to say, its aim is to countervail the damaging effects of cross-examination; and new topics cannot be introduced.

There is one marked disadvantage in re-examination: since the advocate is examining his own witness, he is not allowed to ask leading questions. There is also one marked advantage: if, in cross-examination, questions are asked about part of a conversation or a document, then, so far as is necessary to explain the answers given, the whole conversation or document is admissible, though it would not have been admissible in the first instance. In this way, cross-examination may open the way for new and important evidence.

2 Technique

The technique of re-examination does not call for extended treatment: in principle, *it is simply the insinuation of facts or possibilities* which give a different turn to the answers in cross-examination, but, as the advocate is examining his own witness, a roundabout approach is unnecessary. The real difficulty of re-examination is twofold. The first difficulty is to think of helpful points — which reduces itself to quick thinking and a detailed knowledge of the case. The second difficulty is to frame simple and straightforward questions without leading, for, in view of the complications introduced in cross-examination, there is a tendency for questions in re-examination to be introduced by lengthy preambles and to be appallingly long-winded. The solution to this is, of course, a mastery of the use of language. The examples quoted below show how skilfully an accomplished advocate surmounts these difficulties.

Countering the effect of insinuation

As it is the technique of insinuation which introduces something new in cross-examination, the object of re-examination is, more often than not, to counteract an insinuation. Suppose the evidence-in-chief has raised a certain probability or inference: and afterwards in cross-examination, a fact or a possibility is suggested to weaken this. Re-examination will then be directed either to excluding the suggested fact or possibility, or to bringing out something further to tilt the balance in favour of the original inference.

In the Dickman case,[88] to show that the prisoner had been in the company of the murdered man when they were both about to board the train on which the latter was murdered, a witness named Hepple gave evidence that he had seen them together on the platform and that 'from their demeanour I think they were talking together'. Mitchell-Innes, K.C., asked in cross-examination:

'As far as your hearing went, you cannot say whether they were talking or not?' — 'Except by their demeanour.'

[88]   *Op. cit.,* p. 49.

'So far as your hearing is concerned, you could not tell from your hearing?' — 'Just so. They were eighteen feet from me.'

This was intended to weaken the inference suggested. Tindal Atkinson, K.C., re-examined as follows:

'But could you tell from the movements of their heads whether they were talking together?' — 'Their faces were turned towards one another as being in conversation apparently.'

This is an example of placing a new weight in the scale so as to tilt the balance in the same way as at first.

Here is another example of the same sort, taken from the trial of Vera Boulton at Leeds Assizes (December, 1944). The prisoner worked at a doctor's house, and the doctor's wife gave evidence that while the doctor was out on his morning rounds, the prisoner would have access to the poisons in the surgery. G. H. B. Streatfeild, K.C. (later Streatfeild, J.) asked in cross-examination:

'Did your husband sometimes come back to his surgery in the mornings when he was out on his rounds?' — 'He usually calls, if he has to come in that direction, for any messages.'

'So when he went out on his rounds at 9.30 in the morning he could be expected to call back at any moment?' — 'Yes, at any moment.'

C. Paley Scott, K.C., re-examined as follows:

'You said that your husband usually came in during his rounds. Did you say once or more than once?' — 'Usually only once. He did the left-hand side of the village and then called in on the way to the right side of it . . .'

'So that after he went out the second time he would generally be out to the end of his round?' — 'Yes.'

This re-established the point of uninterrupted access for a substantial period.

The other method — to exclude the possibility suggested — is neatly illustrated in another extract from the same case. The prisoner's little boy had died in a deep coma, and Dr. Platts gave evidence that, as a result of a post-mortem examination, he could find no natural cause of death. (Another witness gave evidence of the presence of poison in the remains.) In cross-examination it was suggested that there might have been a tiny tumour on the brain which could have escaped notice. C. Paley Scott, K.C., re-examined as follows:

'In order to cause death by coma would you expect to find, if it came from a tumour, a very minute one or one easy to find?' — 'I should expect one easy to find.'

'Rather large?' — 'Yes.'

'What would large and small mean, in actual size?' — 'I should say a tumour easily detectable to the naked eye.'

These questions are a model of simplicity and precision.

Counteracting the destructive technique

It is an extremely hard, often impossible task to replace a fallen idol which has been virtually destroyed by confrontation or undermining. Nevertheless, it may be possible to salvage something. The method will be either to insinuate helpful facts — if any — or else, more commonly, to guide the witness to say that he still adheres to his evidence-in-chief. It is difficult to imagine any more fallen idol that Oscar Wilde after Carson's cross-examination: yet he might conceivably have been partially reinstated by a re-examination on these lines:

'Do you prefer to be with young or with old people?' — 'With young people.'

'What is their attraction to you?' — 'They are bright and full of vitality.'

'If they are bright, does it matter to you whether they are intellectual or not?' — 'No.'

'Would it be right to say that young people have a romantic appeal to you?' — 'Yes.'

'Has your interest ever gone beyond that?' — 'No.'

'Has there been anything immoral in your association with these young men?' — 'No.'

'If they say that there has been, what have you to say to that?' — 'They are not speaking the truth.'

'Now, as an artist, do you look upon the world as divided into good and bad, or true and false, or what?' — 'The beautiful and the ugly.'

'How would you describe anything or any person, who repelled your artistic taste?' — 'As ugly.'

'Is that why you used the word "ugly" when my friend cross-examined you?' — 'Yes.'

'Why did you not tell him so at the time?' — 'I was shocked and agitated by the unpleasant suggestion he made.'

This, by the way, is an example of the extensive use of gentle insinuation in re-examination — the re-examiner having to go cautiously because he has no proof from his witness on these point.

As an illustration of guiding a witness to re-affirm the truth of his evidence, the imaginary cross-examination on a previous conviction at p. 105, *ante,* may be used. Re-examination might run like this:

'Have you any interest in the result of this case?' — 'No.'

'Will you gain anything if the plaintiff wins?' — 'No.'

'Is there any reason why you should not speak the truth today?' — 'No.'

'Do you give false evidence without any reason?' — 'No.'

'Whatever you have done in the past, are you telling the truth today or not?' — 'I am telling the truth.'

Fresh evidence elicited in cross-examination

Where fresh evidence has come out in cross-examination (such as Sir Walter Monckton's tentative alibi, at p. 100, *ante*), any of the techniques of cross-examination — confrontation, probing, insinuation — may be brought to bear to modify it. There is only this limitation, that leading questions must not be asked, unless, indeed, the witness has turned hostile.

New evidence made admissible

When new evidence — such as a conversation — has been made admissible by the course of the cross-examination, it will be elicited in the ordinary way as an addition to the examination-in-chief.

Chapter 8

Legal Proof and the Formulation of Arguments

1 Legal proof of facts

No one can listen to the trial of a case where the facts are in dispute — even a small action in the county court — without being struck by the constant appeal of probabilities. At first sight this seems unsatisfactory: surely, it might be objected, certainty is necessary in legal proceedings, and surely certainty can be reached by logical deduction from the known and admitted facts, without arguing about what is likely and unlikely.

The truth is that in practical affairs — such as the proof of facts in legal actions — the mode of reasoning is not the same as it is in scientific subjects, where deductions are drawn from general principles. In geometry, for example, conclusions are drawn by strict logical deduction and are established with *scientific* certainty:[89] in practical affairs the

---

[89] So that I shall not be misunderstood, I point out that the conclusions of a science are certain only if the starting point is valid, but between the starting point and the conclusions there is a deductive process of reasoning which is logically and inherently compelling: in legal

aim is to reach what is sometimes called a moral certainty
— or a state of *conviction* — and in the process the weight
of probabilities, or the convergence of probabilities, plays a
dominating part. Probability, therefore, is an inherent factor
in legal argument, and the appeal to probability is not
accidental but inevitable.

Why is this?

The reason is that in practical affairs we are not
concerned with universal laws of nature, but with
contingent facts, that is to say facts which could have
happened either way. There was no reason in the nature of
things why Wallace should have killed his wife; he might
have done or he might not. Consequently we are thrown
back — so far as direct evidence is not available — on
probabilities in favour of the one alternative or the other.
The philosopher Aristotle perceived this centuries ago, and

reasoning this is not so. I might put it this way: the object
of legal reasoning is to produce certain *belief,* based on
extrinsic evidence; scientific reasoning aims at certain
knowledge, based on intrinsic deductions from principles
— laws of nature — which are either self-evident or
established by induction. As a matter of fact laws of nature
founded on induction are themselves in most cases no
more than probable or approximate, but this does not
really affect the point.

Lord Simonds contrasts scientific and legal proof in
Preston-Jones v. Preston-Jones [1951] 1 All E. R. 124, at
p. 127, where a divorce petition was based on the birth of
a child 360 days after access by the husband: 'The result of
a finding of adultery . . . is . . . to bastardise the child. That
is a matter in which from time out of mind strict proof has
been required. That does not mean, however, that a degree
of proof is demanded such as in a scientific inquiry would
justify the conclusion that such and such an event is
impossible.'

therefore, while his *Logic* was founded on deductive certainty, his *Rhetoric* was found on probability.[90]

It would be wrong, of course, to give the impression that probabilities alone constitute the basis of legal proof. There are, in fact, three modes in which facts can be established:

[90]   Having a great admiration for Aristotle and his gift for exact analysis, I should like to elaborate this in a footnote for those who are interested in fundamental principles. The heart of Aristotle's Logic is the Syllogism, a conclusive form of reasoning like this:

>   All men are mortal. (Major premise.)
>   Africans are men. (Minor premise.)
>   Therefore Africans are mortal. (Conclusion.)

In Rhetoric, Aristotle says, the Syllogism is replaced by the Enthymeme, which differs from the Syllogism by having a *probability* as its major premise, e.g.

>   A man with overwhelming desire to be free from his wife is likely to murder her. (Major premise.)
>   Crippen had an overwhelming desire to be free from his wife. (Minor premise.)
>   Therefore, Crippen was likely to murder her. (Conclusion)

In such cases, the major premise, being obvious, is usually omitted, and thus the term Enthymeme has come to be used (incorrectly) for a Syllogism with a suppressed major premise. Aristotle also quotes (as arguments distinct from the Enthymeme) what he calls the Sign and the Example, which the following examples illustrate:

(i)   Crippen took to flight, and this is a sign of his guilt. (Sign.)

(ii) It is said, how could Wallace murder his wife without his clothing being covered with blood? But there was a case in the nineteenth century where a man committed a murder while completely naked. (Example.)

The difference between these three is only one of rhetorical form (Example can be most impressive) and in the text I refer to all three alike as probabilities.

(i)   Direct evidence — that is to say, the facts are proved
        by an eyewitness (including in this any admissible
        confessions by an accused person);

(ii)   Logical deduction from direct evidence;

(iii)   Probable inferences, based on the facts proved by
        direct evidence or directly deduced from those facts.

To illustrate this let us take a specimen case where a dead
body is found with a knife buried in its back. The face has
not been injured, and is identified by a wife or husband or
other person who knew the dead man very well.

    Then:

(i)   The fact that a certain person is dead as the result of
        a knife wound is established by direct evidence.

(ii)   By strict deduction, it is established that the knife
        wound was inflicted by another person, because the
        deceased could not have reached round to stab
        himself.

(iii)   The identity of the murderer is left to be established
        by probable inference from a great mass of
        surrounding circumstances (of which direct evidence
        is given). (Such a mass of evidence leading to a
        probable inference is, of course, what we know as
        circumstantial evidence.)

It will be clear that the zone of probable inference embraces
nearly everything which is likely to be disputed. In a case
of this sort, the facts proved by direct evidence will, in the
main, be common ground. If, in any case, the direct
evidence is disputed, on the ground that the witness is
mistaken or lying, probability comes in again from another
angle, to determine the veracity or accuracy of the witness,
and this is especially the case where the witnesses on
opposite sides do not agree.

    It is fair to say, therefore, that in any question of
disputed fact the arguments will be based on probability.

Standard of proof in civil cases

The standard of proof in civil cases has been much discussed in actions for negligence where there is no direct proof of negligent acts or omissions.[91] The burden of proof is, of course, on the plaintiff. An initial question for the court is whether there is *sufficient* evidence on which the court or a jury can (though it is not bound to do so) find in favour of the plaintiff. It has been said that it is not enough to offer a 'pure conjecture', there must be a 'reasonable inference', that is to say something more weighty than a mere possibility. Lord Macmillan says:

> 'If nothing has been proved to render more probable any one of two or more theories . . . , then the plaintiff . . . has left the case in equilibrium and the Court is not entitled to incline the balance one way or the other . . . The dividing line between conjecture and inference is often a very difficult one to draw. A conjecture may be plausible, but it is of no legal value, for its essence is that it is a mere guess. An inference in the legal sense, on the other hand, is a deduction from the evidence, and if it is a reasonable deduction it may have the validity of legal proof . . . The cogency of a legal inference may vary between practical certainty and reasonable probability.'

If we turn now to the usual type of case where there is direct evidence and probable inferences (or one or other of them) on both sides, the question becomes one of the *weight* of evidence, not of sufficiency. It is the duty of the court or jury to decide the issues according to the weight of the evidence, and an appeal lies if it fails to do so. When can it be said that there is a superior weight of evidence on one side, so as to amount to firm legal proof? The answer is given in a celebrated judgment of Lord Mansfield:

[91]   *Jones v. Great Western Railway* (1931) 144 L.T. 194, pp. 201-202. The whole case is worth reading. The principle set out in the text is the theoretical basis of the maxim *Res Ipsa Loquitur,* which applies when the facts of the accident, in themselves, give rise to a probable inference.

'As mathematical and absolute certainty is seldom to be attained in human affairs, reason and public utility require that judges and all mankind in forming their opinion of the truth of facts should be regulated by the superior number of probabilities on the one side or the other.'

That is to say, a civil case is decided according to the *balance* of the probabilities, not indeed by counting the number of arguments on each side — far from it — but by assessing which version is more likely, having regard to the whole of the facts and the suggested inferences arising from them. The task of the advocate, in formulating his argument, is to bring to bear a superior weight of probability.

Standard of proof in criminal cases

The standard of proof in a criminal case is necessarily much higher — the guilt of the prisoner has to be proved beyond all reasonable doubt. The point may be expressed in this way: a mere balance of probabilities is enough in a civil action, but in a criminal case the probabilities must *converge* to establish the guilt of the prisoner with complete moral certainty. Lord Wright said in his summing-up in the Wallace case:[92]

'If every matter relied on as circumstantial is equally or substantially consistent both with the guilt or innocence of the prisoner, the multiplication of these instances may not take you any further in coming to a conclusion of guilt.'

[92]   *Trial of Wallace,* p. 286. Any words of Lord Wright on these fundamental principles have peculiar weight as he, more than any other English judge, has explored the fundamental principles of our law. We see many works by writers with Germanic names on the so-called 'philosophy of law'; an English law student will be well-advised to ignore these spider's webs spun out of unrealities and to study, instead, the speeches of Lord Wright and Lord Macmillan.

The addition of probabilities is not enough in a criminal case: it is not enough that there should be a series of parallel lines in a given direction, they must converge to a fixed point.

The trial of Wallace is a remarkable example of a case where the civil standard of proof was reached, but not the criminal standard; and this was the ground on which the conviction was quashed by the Court of Criminal Appeal.

It follows from these remarks that the defending advocate has a choice of tactics: he may attempt to establish a great weight of probability, founded on the facts, in favour of the prisoner's innocence, or he may content himself with drawing a vivid picture of a reasonable possibility consistent with innocence. Sometimes the two methods may be combined.

2 Arguments on the facts

The arguments are the heart of the speeches, and therefore must be formulated right at the start. The material for the arguments is drawn from the advocate's knowledge of mankind and affairs, and its selection is a matter for the exercise of practical judgment.

As an aid to the formulation of arguments, it may be useful to reflect on the established facts from certain general points of view. For instance, useful starting points can be obtained from consideration of the motives and drawbacks of an action; from opportunity and method; from causes and effects; from antecedent and subsequent conduct or events; and from the collateral circumstances which distinguish a particular act or happening.[93] In nearly every legal

---

[93]   General points of view of this kind — used as matrices for arguments — are known in Rhetoric as the Topics: I have selected those which are relevant to legal argument.

argument, the facts are approached from one or another of these angles.

Legal speeches tend to bristle with arguments, big and little; in a narrative of the facts, every fact is made to speak and to point more or less in the desired direction. It is the duty of an advocate, however, to be selective: the main points should stand out clearly; the subsidiary arguments should remain in the background, without being over-stressed; weak arguments should be rejected altogether. A speech which contains a long catalogue of points good and bad, important and trivial, carries little conviction: an effective speech leaves the court or jury in no doubt about the key-arguments, and uses the subsidiary points to strengthen these.

Here are two examples of arguments from probability: both taken from the case of Dr. Crippen. (Crippen poisoned his wife in order to be free to marry Miss Le Neve, and buried her remains in his cellar. When inquiries were made about the whereabouts of his missing wife, he took to flight with Miss Le Neve, disguised as a boy. The cellar was then investigated and the remains discovered; a wireless message was sent and Crippen was arrested on board ship. Crippen denied that the remains were those of his wife and said he had no knowledge of their presence; it should also be noted that he had circulated stories that his wife had gone to America and died there, but at the time of the trial he said that he believed she had left him for another man.)

(i)   Flight, especially when coupled with concealment of identity, raises a strong probability of guilt.

(ii)   A body is unlikely to be buried in a man's cellar without his knowledge.

These are two arguments for the prosecution: it was incumbent on the defence to answer them in some way. Now there are several courses which may be taken in refuting an argument based on probability. *The facts on which it rests may of course be denied* (this was not possible here, except that in regard to the second point it was contended without success that the remains might date from before Crippen's occupation of the house). Then, *the probability* urged on the other side *may be denied*. The strongest argument of all is *to raise a counter-probability*. This was what the defence did here, quite forcibly, with regard to the flight.

Answer to (i). Flight may have been an act of folly with knowledge of all the suspicions raised, but still consistent with innocence. The main thing is, what was the reason for flight? Incidental details such as disguise count for little if the flight itself is explained. (So far, counsel has shown only a *reasonable possibility*, which is of course a sufficient answer to a probable argument in a *criminal* case. He now turns his argument into a probability.) 'He did what innocent men, threatened with a charge, have done before.'

With regard to the second argument, it was sufficient, of course, to establish a reasonable possibility that remains of a body might be buried in Crippen's cellar without his knowledge, and this the defence counsel tried to do, first by suggesting that they might date from before he took the house, then by saying (not a convincing point) that after all Crippen was often away from the house for long periods. Finally he built up, very ingeniously, a counter-probability based on the fact that, before Crippen's flight and the discovery of the remains, Crippen and a detective officer went over the house together and stood in the cellar.

Answer to (ii). Would he stand in the cellar with the detective inspector without turning a hair, if he knew that his wife's remains were buried there?

These general remarks should give some indication of the methods followed both in formulating arguments and in refuting them. In conclusion, a summary of Sir Richard Muir's complete opening in the Crippen case is given below.[94] A prosecutor in a criminal case must not only bring to bear the superior weight of evidence required in a civil case. In bringing out his points he must seek to exclude, one by one, possible explanations of damaging facts which may be suggested: so that finally, as the speech concludes, no reasonable explanation remains open which is consistent with the prisoner's innocence.

1.   *State of affairs preceding the crime.* At the material time Crippen was in love with Miss Le Neve, estranged from his wife, and in need of money which was largely in the name of his wife. (*Antecedents.*)

2.   His wife and his want of money were obstacles in the way of his love for Miss Le Neve. The death of his wife would remove both. (*Motives.*)

3.   Mrs. Crippen was last seen on 31st January, when some friends came to dinner. She was then in good health. She vanished, but left behind her dresses and jewellery. (*Opportunity.*)

4.   The doctor gave false reasons for her disappearance. Her friends were suspicious and started police inquiries. (*Consequences.*)

5.   He took flight with Le Neve (disguised as a boy). (*Consequences.*)

6.   The remains were found buried in the cellar of the house. They had been identified by certain characteristics as the remains of Mrs. Crippen. Crippen alone had the opportunity to put the remains there. (*Opportunity.*)

7.   He was arrested, and gave no explanation of his flight. (*Consequences.*)

---

[94]   *The Trial of Crippen,* pp. 3 et seq. I also strongly recommend a study of the arguments of the Dean of Faculty and the Solicitor-General in the Arran case.

8.   Finally, the remains contained a fatal dose of hyoscin; and Crippen had bought hyoscin. (*Opportunity and method.*)

9.   The jury had to ask: What became of Mrs. Crippen? Were the remains hers? If so, what was the explanation of how they got here? (Implied inference: *There is no explanation consistent with Crippen's innocence.*)

3 Arguments on the law

Arguments on questions of law are a very different matter from arguments on the facts. No questions of probability arise here, for law is a science, that is to say a body of general principles, though it is not an exact science like mathematics.

It is worth considering the genesis of principles of law.

The first stage is that a judge decides a case. Assuming that there are no precedents or other material — and there was not a great deal in the early days of the law — he decides according to what he believes to be objective standards of justice and the spirit of the common law.

From a series of such cases general principles emerge. This is the second stage.

In the third stage ample sources are available — mostly decided cases, perhaps partly statute law. The duty of the judge is then to decide the case according to settled principles, which means that he must select the principles which are appropriate, generally from a line of cases, distinguishing other lines of cases as falling outside the relevant principle. At the same time he may re-state or modify the principle in the light of new factors which were not taken into account by his predecessors, or in view of the obsolescence of older factors.

According to this interpretation, law is an inductive science, building up flexible principles of objective justice on the basis of stubborn fact.

The enunciation of principles

It is a very bad fallacy in legal argument to rely on a case which is said to be 'on all fours' with that which is being decided. The court is not concerned at all with the facts of another case, except so far as they throw light on principles. The law reports are full of cases which are 'on all fours' with one another, but were decided in the opposite way — because their resemblance was apparent only and not real.[95]

An advocate who is presenting an argument of law hopes that his submissions will form the foundation of the judgment of the court. Therefore the arguments should be sound and not specious, and formulated on much the same lines as the judge would formulate them in his judgment. The arguments of Sir John Simon are brilliant models of this approach.

The first stage, therefore, is to formulate the general propositions of law which the court is invited to accept.

The next stage is to offer an array of cases — or it may be only one or two — in support of these propositions. If cases have to be distinguished, they should be distinguished on principle, so as to show a clear dividing line with groups of decisions on each side of it. The only exception ('distinguishing on the facts') is where it is submitted that a particular case or group of cases represents an anomaly, which is not consistent with principle, but must be followed on grounds of authority, though it ought not to be extended.

Failing any principle which governs the case, the best line is the argument from analogy, a fertile source of arguments, which is in fact the main builder of our common law: for the whole of the law of tort and contract developed in the Middle Ages from the prototype of

[95]   See the remarks of Lord Loreburn, L.C. in *McCartan v. Belfast Commissioners* (1911) 2 I.R. at p. 145.

Trespass, partly on the initiative of the courts and partly under the influence of the statute *In Consimili Casu*. An imaginary example (unlikely to succeed) may be taken from the controversial 'right to privacy', as where a man brings an action because his photograph has been taken by the press without his permission. It might be said:

> An action lies for libel, which consists in injuring a man's reputation. The action rests on the right to reputation. Just as a man has a right to his own reputation, restricted only by the public interest, so also he has a right not to have his privacy impinged upon, except for reasons of public interest; and just as an action lies for the infringement of the right to reputation, so also an action ought to lie for infringement of the right to privacy.

This is a rather bold analogy, but an effective illustration of the type of argument: usually it does not leap so far.

Questions of degree or of discretion

Often the problem is not so much to determine the correct principles of law as to apply them to the facts of the case: and this may involve questions of *degree,* such as whether certain proved omissions were 'negligent', or whether a certain machine was 'dangerous'. Such a problem is individual to the particular case, it is really a question of *interpreting* the facts in the light of known standards of law. The judge has to decide according to his practical judgment, and the proper course in argument is to suggest the sort of considerations, on the facts of the case, which will guide him to a sound conclusion. Similar observations apply to discretionary matters, such as the apportionment of damages between joint tortfeasors.

The construction of statutes and documents

By convention, the construction of a statute or a document is a question of law for the court, though in reality it is a question of fact — or the interpretation of fact — dependent on the facts of the individual case, and the decision in one case is no more than a general guide in deciding another. The judge decides according to his own practical judgment, according to the various indications in the document: probabilities come into play here, as in no other arguments of law.[96]

The groundwork in such a case is to outline the scheme and background of the statute or document. The rest of the argument will be taken up with drawing attention to the sort of considerations in the document on which the judge may act; and also to drawing out the various probabilities which can be raised in favour of the construction contended for.

Top quality examples of arguments of law may be found in dissenting opinions in the House of Lords.[96a]

---

[96]   'To decide upon proven probabilities is not to guess but to adjudicate': per Lord Atkin in *Perrin v. Morgan* [1943] A.C. 399 at p. 414 (construction of a home-made will).

[96a] See *Liversidge v. Anderson* (1941) 3 All E.R. 338 (Atkin); *Midland Silicones v. Scrutton* (1962) 1 All E.R. 1 (Denning); *Shelley v. L.C.C.* (1948) 2 All E.R. 898 (du Parcq); *London Graving Rock v. Horton* (1951) 2 All E.R. 1 (Reid).

Chapter 9

The Speeches

1 The construction and arrangement of a speech

Having dealt with the formulation of the arguments, we come to the construction of the speeches in which they are to be put forward.

A speech consists of two essential parts:[97]

(i)   *The Statement,* that is to say the statement and explanation of what is to be proved.

(ii)   *The Proof,* that is to say the arguments in support.

In a legal speech, the *statement* is usually quite short: e.g. 'The case for the prosecution is that Dr. Crippen poisoned his wife with hyoscin, and afterwards disposed of her body by dismembering it and burying the remains in his cellar.' In a complicated civil action, however, such as an action for libel or malicious prosecution, the issues will be more complex, and may have to be explained at some length before going on to the evidence in support. (For an

[97]   In this analysis I follow Aristotle (*Rhetoric,* III, xiii-xix), whose explanation of the divisions of the speech is still the clearest available.

example, see the opening by Mr. G. O. Slade, K.C., in *The Laski Libel Action.*)

The *proof* falls into two divisions, which need not, of course, follow one another consecutively, but may be intermingled. The first division consists of the arguments in support of one's own case; the second is the refutation of the argument advanced, or likely to be advanced, on the other side. The sources and nature of these arguments were indicated in the last chapter. Two short observations may be added, almost in the words of Aristotle. The first is that arguments ought not, in a legal speech, to be set out in a continuous sequence, but worked in here and there. The second is that an argument may be refuted in two ways: either by objecting to its validity on one ground or another, or by setting up a counter-argument.

In addition to these essential components — which must always be present — a speech may also contain:

(i)   *An Introduction,* sometimes known as the Exordium or Proemium; and

(ii)   *A Peroration,* also described as the Epilogue or the Recapitulation.

If the subject is plain and short, there is no need for an introduction. Its object is to pave the way, as it were, for the main speech. Thus in his introduction a speaker seeks chiefly to arouse interest, in order that attention may be given to his arguments; he seeks also to remove prejudices, and to make his audience favourably disposed towards the case he is about to present. The introduction is therefore important in addressing a jury, above all in removing prejudices, and it is perhaps the most delicate part of the speech for the defence in a criminal case. Sir Walter Monckton aroused the interest of the jury, in his defence of Ley, by stressing the *mysterious* nature of the case, which at once made the jury attentive. However, even before a judge, an introduction may sometimes be useful; thus the Court of Appeal will listen more attentively if they are to consider an important point of law; and the House of Lords themselves may have to be led gently into an iconoclastic mood if their Lordships are to be invited to destroy an old and wayward precedent.

The aims of the introduction, then, are to arouse interest and attention; to excite favourable feelings and to allay prejudices; and finally, either to magnify the issues by lifting them to a higher plane, or to minimise their importance. If in any case these objects are unnecessary, at least a few well-chosen preliminary words may make it easier to follow the speech.

The object of the peroration is to bring the speech to a climax and drive home the essential arguments, at the same time arousing the feelings to which the facts of the case naturally give rise: such as the desire to see justice done where the prisoner is proved to have committed a deliberate and callous murder. Here, as an example, is the peroration of the Solicitor-General for Scotland (Lord Stormonth Darling) in his speech for the prosecution in the Arran case:[98]

> 'Gentlemen, if you come to the conclusion, as I have done,[99] that Laurie's was the hand which inflicted the death blow, then all his subsequent conduct is explained. The character and nature of the ground and the other circumstances I have mentioned all point clearly and conclusively to the fact that Rose was killed by the accused. It is to that conclusion that I reluctantly and sorrowfully, yet distinctly and clearly, ask you to come. Gentlemen, it is beyond all reasonable doubt that the accused is guilty of this murder, and I ask you for your verdict accordingly.'

If a speech is long and complicated, some such climax is necessary, to give a finishing touch and drive home the

---

[98] *Op. cit.,* p. 199.
[99] The Solicitor-General ought not, of course, to have expressed his own personal opinion on the case: see p. 10, *ante.*

conclusion. In a short speech, free from complication, the peroration may be dispensed with.

The use of narrative

Some authorities regard the narrative of the facts as a distinct part of the speech. In fact, however, narrative is used at every stage. Part of the story is often told to explain the issues: this consists as a rule of the facts which are common ground. The rest of the narrative is broken into stages and spread out over the arguments. As each stage of the story is concluded, an argument is based on it, or often enough just implied, so that the facts are made to speak for themselves.

Narrative should always be clear and orderly. It should also arouse interest, by telling the story in a vivid and imaginative way, and bringing out the character and emotional behaviour of the chief actors. However, the advocate should not enter into excessive detail, but confine himself to the essential facts required to explain and prove the case. In general, narrative is more important in a speech for the plaintiff or the prosecution than it is for the defence, though the defence may wish to go over the story phase by phase to give it a different colour.

The complete speech

A complete speech will therefore consist of:
(i)   An Introduction.
(ii)   The Statement of the Issues.
(iii)   The Proof.
(iv)   The Peroration.
Narrative will be spread throughout the speech.

As a general illustration, here is the outline of the speech of Anthony Hawke, K.C. (prosecuting) in the trial of Ley and Smith.[100]

Introduction (a very simple one)

1. Ley and Smith are charged with murder.

Explanatory Narrative

2. The dead body of Mudie was found in a chalk pit in Surrey. He had been strangled with a rope. There was no mud on his shoes, and he must have been carried there.

Statement

3. The Crown will contend that Mudie was murdered at the London house of Ley, and that both Ley and Smith were concerned in the murder.

Proof

4. Ley was jealous of Mrs. Brooks' supposed association with other men.
5. This jealousy fixed itself (without any justification) on Mudie.
6. Ley plotted with Smith and other men (all paid by him) to have Mudie brought to his house and tied up there.
7. Ley and Smith were left there alone with Mudie tied up in a chair.
8. The body was found two days later at the chalk pit.
9. Smith had been seen reconnoitring the chalk pit before the murder.

Peroration

10. There was cogent evidence that both Ley and Smith were together at the house, engaged in a joint enterprise which resulted in murder.

[100] *Op. cit.,* pp. 3-21. This sort of note should be a sufficient basis for an extempore speech.

2 Other elements in a good speech

The appeal to the emotions

It is sometimes said that an appeal to the emotions is out of place in the law courts, as detracting from objectivity and reason. This is a reaction against the artificial oratory of the eighteenth and early nineteenth centuries, and is true up to a point.

It is essential, nevertheless, that the intelligence *and the will* of the listener should be brought to work in conjunction in favour of the advocate: reasons drawn from the facts influence the intelligence and at the same time the natural feelings aroused by the facts influence the will. In an earlier chapter a contrast was drawn between the logical certitude attained in mathematics and the moral certitude attained in practical affairs. The intellect is *forced* to accept a logical conclusion, such as the proof of a theorem in geometry: but it is never forced to accept a belief prompted by extrinsic evidence — a moral certitude — and for complete *conviction* in a matter of this kind the assent of the will is needed. Hence, the appeal to the intellect and the will must go together, but a real advocate will seek to arouse only those feelings which are naturally prompted by the facts of the case and will avoid artificiality.

In this connection the advocate has two roles. First, he must dispel antagonistic feelings or prejudices, which will prevent his arguments from receiving a fair hearing: the main place for this is in the introduction, but care must be taken throughout the whole case not to do anything which will arouse antagonism in the judge or jury.

The second task is to build up favourable feelings, and this is done mainly by causing the facts to speak to the will in the same way as they speak to the intelligence. Thus villainy should be exposed in such a manner as to prompt indignation; or sympathy may be aroused for the dilemma of an honourable man placed in an impossible position, or for the cruel sufferings which a woman has undergone, though partly through her own fault.[101]

The appeal to the emotions is naturally more prominent in addressing a jury, but it is not to be ignored in other cases. A judge may be reluctant to decide a question of law, or to take an original line, and his reluctance must be overcome. Again, a really good judge has a love of justice if he has no other emotion: Lord Atkin had a brilliant gift for making law at all times the servant of justice, in spite of difficulties and technicalities which seemed to make this impossible. Thus, the case must appeal to the judge's sense of justice, as well as to his reason.

Style and delivery

The essence both of good style and of good delivery is clearness, so that the case is understood. If, over and above this, it is possible to add a varied and graceful style and a pleasant and varied delivery, the speech will interest and please the listener and so will be more likely to convince. Delivery is a matter of elocution and voice development, which is too big to be explained here — even if the author were competent to do so. Style is likewise a large subject. Aristotle thought that a mixture of the familiar and unfamiliar was important: certainly an unfamiliar word or phrase or picture here and there, to relieve the monotony of everyday language, adds to the charm of the speech. Contrast in the build-up of sentences is also necessary, as too many involved phrases are tedious, while short sentences in succession may be jerky. Frequent change from one to the other is the key to smoothness and balance. The

---

[101] Cf. the defence of Mme. Fahmy by Marshall Hall and the defence of Malcolm by Sir John Simon: Marjoribanks, *Life of Marshall Hall,* pp. 364 et seq., 434 et seq. Marshall Hall owes his title as a great advocate to his mastery of this branch of oratory, but it may be noted that when the occasion arose Sir John Simon was his equal.

use of figures of speech — similes, metaphors and the like — requires great care. Arguments and narrative can often be illuminated by a vivid picture: on the other hand, dead and well-worn metaphors will irritate any listener whose taste is critical, and, moreover, they have lost their vivid and pictorial value. It is in metaphor, more than in any other context, that the introduction of something unfamiliar but striking may carry unexpected force: as in Marshall Hall's famous picture of Justice holding the scales, where the presumption of innocence is an invisible weight thrown into the balance.[102] An advocate who introduces metaphor must be original.

The characteristics of a good speech

The characteristics of a good speech are threefold:

(i)   *To interest,* especially by striking the right note in the introduction and by vividness in the narrative, and also by grace of style and delivery.

(ii)   *To prove,* by clear exposition and argument, which appeal to the intellect.

(iii)   *To convince,* by breaking down the resistance of the will and rendering it favourable. This process starts with the note struck in the introduction, is heightened by the narrative, and brought to a climax in the peroration.

3 The order of the speeches

(i) Civil actions

If the case is tried by jury, the first step is for junior counsel for the plaintiff to 'open the pleadings', that is to inform the jury briefly of the issues raised by the pleadings.

The right to begin rests with the plaintiff if, on the pleadings, the burden of proving any of the issues (even the

---

[102]   E.g. *Trial of the Seddons,* pp. 331-332.

amount of damages) rests on him. Otherwise the defendant has the right to begin. For convenience, it will be assumed in the following paragraph that it is the plaintiff who begins: if the defendant begins, the order of the speeches is the same, except that the defendant starts.

The plaintiff's counsel makes his opening speech and calls his witnesses. If the defendant is not calling witnesses, the plaintiff's counsel then sums up and the defendant replies. If the defendant is calling witnesses, he opens his case, calls the witnesses and sums up; and the plaintiff then makes his speech in reply, instead of summing up at the conclusion of his own evidence.

In the county court the order is much the same, except that the defendant is not entitled to make a second speech except at the judge's discretion: consequently, the usual practice is for the defendant to call his witnesses first and make his speech afterwards.

(ii) Criminal cases

The prosecutor opens and calls his witnesses. If the defence is calling no witnesses, the prosecutor then sums up, and the defendant addresses the jury. If the defence is calling no witnesses other than the prisoner and witnesses of character, the order is unchanged, except that these witnesses are interposed between the prosecution witnesses and the summing-up for the prosecution; so that the defence still has the right to the last word. If the defence is calling witnesses to the facts (other than the prisoner), the order is as follows: prosecutor opens and calls his witnesses; defendant's counsel opens, call his witnesses and sums up; finally prosecutor replies (but this right is not always exercised, at any rate on circuit).

Exceptionally, the Attorney-General or the Solicitor-General, if prosecuting in person, always has the right to reply.

If the prisoner is found guilty, then after formal evidence of any previous convictions his counsel may address the judge in mitigation.

4 The opening

The opening of a case has the same key-position as the evidence-in-chief: the case pivots round it, and the opening must be prepared thoroughly, Introduction, Statement, Proof, and Peroration are all important. In the introduction, it may be necessary to create the right atmosphere from the start, so that the plaintiff or prosecutor has the full advantage of the first word. Narrative is also a leading factor in the opening, to ensure that the court or jury has a firm grasp of the essential background of the case.

An advocate must not state facts in his opening unless he is calling witnesses to prove them. Therefore, openings are pitched moderately, in case witnesses do not come up to expectation.

It is a firm rule of professional ethics that a prosecuting counsel must be fair. While bringing out the full force of the adverse evidence he must also draw attention to any facts which tell in favour of the prisoner and must not press for a conviction unless justified by the evidence.

The illustration which follows is a model of conciseness, simplicity and moderation, while the facts are clearly stated and allowed to speak for themselves. It is the opening address of C. Paley Scott, K.C., prosecuting in the case of Vera Boulton at Leeds Assizes.[103]

---

[103]   I have not altered the punctuation of the shorthand writer, which brings out the raciness of the spoken word. I have, however, italicised those portions of the narrative which convey arguments as distinct from facts.

This illustration has been chosen, I may say, partly because it is not too long, and partly because it is not a famous or unusual case, but one taken straight from everyday circuit practice.

Introduction and Statement combined

Mr. Paley Scott: 'May it please your Lordship, Members of the Jury, you have just heard the charge against this defendant is that of wilful murder, and the person she is alleged to have murdered is her own son, aged 5½ years. The nature of the allegation against her, that which the prosecution set out to prove, is that she killed that child by a gross and fatal over-dose of a well-known sleeping drug (the technical name of which is pheno barbitone, and the popular name of which is luminal) administered about the 23rd July this year.

'It is a drug in common use, and in proper doses can be taken apparently without harm; it is a poison; it is sold only in bottles that are labelled "Poison", and it should only, of course, be taken upon a doctor's prescription.

'There is no actual direct evidence that she ever administered this drug at all. You will be asked, when you have heard the evidence, to infer that fact from a rather remarkable sequence of facts that will be proved, and I will shortly outline to you what those facts are.'

Narrative: First Stage

'This prisoner lives at Ampleforth, about 20 miles from York, a place very much in the depth of the country. This little boy had to be taken to the York County Hospital about two years ago, where he had a double mastoid operation, an operation to a part of both ears, and in June of this year he was in hospital again and had some further operative or exploratory operation, at any rate upon one mastoid, but by the 11th June he was able to be discharged, apparently quite all right.

'As a result of this treatment I think the boy was a little deaf — rather hard of hearing, but otherwise he appeared to be in perfect health, and within two or three days the defendant complained to the village doctor, Dr. Vidal, who had been attending the boy, that the child was suffering from dizzy fits, that he now and then fell down, and that he showed signs of sleepiness, and accordingly, on the 15th June, Dr. Vidal drove the boy into York. He was then in either a very heavy sleep or in what is known as a coma.

'Dr. Vidal drove the boy to a Dr. Thomas in York, who was the doctor who had operated upon him for mastoid, and you can well understand there was the thought in the minds of the doctors that something might have been left as a result of that treatment which caused, perhaps, a little pressure on the brain or something of that sort which might account for the child's condition.

'He was sent by Dr. Thomas and Dr. Vidal into the Hospital again; he arrived there about a quarter past two; the defendant had been taken over with him, and he remained in the deep sleep or coma for some thirty hours. The mother, the defendant, speaking to a nurse at the Hospital, said that he had been dizzy and that he had fallen into the coma at about ten o'clock that morning. I think the thirty hours is reckoned, therefore, from that time of 10 o'clock.

'By the 20th June the boy was practically normal; after he came round there had been no further symptom of anything wrong, and on the 22nd June his mother visited him. She left at about three o'clock and by a quarter past three the boy was again in a deep coma. He did not come to on that occasion for fifteen hours. Having come round he became gradually normal again, and seemed to have nothing that anyone could discover the matter with him.

'On the 29th June the mother again visited him, and on this occasion, after she had left, he fell at once into a coma and so remained for no less than forty hours. By the 5th July the boy appeared to be practically himself again and was even able to get up and run about in the ward, but on Sunday, 9th July, his mother visited him again and towards the end of her visit she drew the nurse's attention to the fact that he was apparently beginning to get drowsy, and he fell into a sleep before she left on that occasion, and in that sleep he remained again for fifteen hours.

'The doctors were puzzled by the case, and when the defendant came again Dr. Blackwood, who was Dr. Thomas's assistant, and who was in charge of the case, spoke to the mother (this was on the 12th July, three days after the last visit) and asked whether she had given the child anything to eat while she was there. She admitted that she had given the child sweets, and the doctor told her that she was to give him nothing at all, either to eat or drink.

'Certain instructions were also given by the doctor to the nurses in charge of the ward, and as a result of that Mrs. Boulton, the defendant, was closely watched throughout her visit on that day. It is fair to say, and right that I should tell you, that so far as the nurses know defendant did not know that she was being watched. There were a number of other patients in the ward, who would have an opportunity of seeing, and she had been definitely told to give the child nothing. After she left the child was perfectly normal.'

'She came again on Sunday, 16th July; she was again watched; she was not seen to give the child anything, and after her visit the child was perfectly normal. On the 19th July she called again. By some oversight no person watched on that occasion, but the child was again normal after her visit, and on the 21st July, the child being, so far as those in the hosiptal could tell, perfectly recovered, he was released from the hospital and Dr. Vidal drove him home to Ampleforth, handed him over to the defendant and said: "Here he is; he's quite all right again."'

First Argument

'There is, up to that point, if there were no other evidence, you may think, reason, at any rate, to suspect that those three periods of unconsciousness, for which no medical reason could be assigned, were in some way connected with the mother's visits; but the evidence does not quite stop there, because certain patients in the hospital and persons visiting patients in the hospital on Sunday the 9th July (the last occasion when I told you the child had had a coma or sleeping fit after the mother's visit; the occasion when it began actually while the mother was still there) observed certain things.'

Narrative: Second Stage; Second Argument

'A Mr. Rollason was lying in bed, a patient at that time, exactly opposite to where the child was, and he had seen the child before and he had seen the mother before; he knew her by sight; he saw her arrive on that day, and later he saw her give the boy something; he saw the boy swallow it. It appeared rather as if it was a sweet, because it had been wrapped in a piece of paper, and he saw the child lick the paper after he had eaten the sweet. *Then rather an odd thing; the defendant turned round, and of course would see that Mr. Rollason was watching, and she said: "That was a sweet". What else would anybody expect it to be, and what need, if no improper thing had been given, you may think, for a parent visiting a child in hospital to explain, after giving what apparently was a sweet, "That was a sweet".*

'Other people noticed rather more than Mr. Rollason noticed. He will tell you that some little time later the defendant said: "Look, his eyes are going funny", and Mr. Rollason said: "You should tell the nurse", and she did, and within half an hour the child was in the deep sleep that I told you about.

'Mrs. Rollason was also there, and she noticed something which you may think happened just before the sweet was given. She noticed the defendant give the boy something — put something into the boy's mouth — and at once give him a drink from the bottle that stood on the locker by the bedside — lemonade or something. Then she saw the defendant pick up the packet of sweets and give it to the boy, and heard her say to him: "Don't eat them all at once". It may be it was one of those sweets that Mr. Rollason saw the boy eating.

'A Mr. Reid was a patient in the same ward (Ward No. 10), and all he noticed apparently given to the boy was a drink of lemonade, soon after which he began to become sleepy, but Mr. Reid's wife (who was visiting him) saw rather more. *She saw the defendant give the boy something into his hand; she saw him put it into his mouth; she saw him pull a wry face and she heard him say: "It's nasty, mummy"* — you will be told that tablets of luminal have *rather a bitter taste — and she heard the mother say: "Don't chump it; swallow it,* and I will give you a drink of lemonade", and she saw the mother give the boy a drink of lemonade, *and soon after the boy began to become "sleepyfied".*

Narrative: Third Stage; Third Argument

'The boy had been brought home, I told you, on the 21st July. Of course, Dr. Vidal went more than once to see the boy, and at some time that I cannot quite tell you — I think it was on the 23rd or 24th July — the boy had become so deeply asleep that it was impossible to arouse him, and Mrs. Vidal went down on the 24th July to administer an enema to the boy, whose bowels had not been moved — he was completely unconscious at that time, and on the 25th July Dr. Vidal drove the defendant and the boy, still deeply unconscious (indeed he never became conscious again) to the York County Hospital. You will be told the mother appeared to be distressed at the child's condition; the coma was markedly worse than those which had preceded it; there were symptoms which had not previously been present, or at any rate not previously noted; *the ordinary reflexes, as they are called were completely absent — they had been present in the earlier terms of long periods of sleep — and it was associated with stertorous breathing, both symptoms of the poisonous virtues of this drug.*

'A sample of spinal fluid was drawn from the boy, to see if it gave any clue to this mysterious condition, but on the 26th July his temperature suddenly rose rapidly to 103 and he died that day without recovering consciousness.

'On the 28th July a post-mortem was held and nothing whatever was found to account for death. Those who held it were particular to observe the condition at the place where the mastoid operations had taken place; there was nothing there which could possibly account for the child's condition, and being unable to determine the cause of death the sample of spinal fluid and certain parts of the internal organs of the child were removed and were sent to an analyst at Sheffield, together also with a sample of the child's water, which would have to be drawn from it, I think, by the use of a catheter, and he examined those things. He did not find enough to determine the precise drug that was present, but *he found barbituric acid reactions. That is an acid which is found not only in pheno-barbitone or luminal, but also in barbitone, commonly called veronal.*

'These — except what he had used up in the experiments — were sent by him to the Senior Home Office Analyst, Dr. Roche Lynch, for further examination and analysis. The remains of those things were sent, an order was obtained for the exhumation of the body, and some parts of the body, and a large part of the contents of the brain, were sent to Dr. Roche Lynch.

'He made a very thorough and full examination and analysis. I will not tell you anything of the details now; you will have to hear those when Dr. Roche Lynch goes into the witness box. It is sufficient to say that he identified the barbiturate as being pheno-barbitone or luminal; he was able to examine the crystals and *he found what was, to him, conclusive evidence of a gross overdose of that drug.*

'The drug is sold in tablets of one grain and half a grain — you can get either — and 15 grains is the smallest known fatal does for an adult. Anything from thirty to sixty grains is considered to be a fatal dose. People, of course, differ very much in their tolerance for drugs of this kind; some people can stand, without fatal effect, a great deal more than others. A dose of luminal for a child of 5½ years would not be more than about a third of an adult dose — the adult dose is two grains. You will therefore be told that five grains might be a fatal dose for a boy of five years of age — 15 to 20 grains almost certainly would.

'How could this woman have procured a drug of this sort — it is not a drug, I imagine, that chemists would sell except either to a doctor or to a person who had a doctor's prescription for it, but the defendant had, from about the end of May until 17th July (that was towards the end of the child's stay in hospital) been the daily servant at Dr. Vidal's house. *One of her duties there had been to sweep out the surgery; she had free access to it; it was not kept locked, so she could have gone in at any time, and the drugs (even those kept in the bottles labelled "Poison", as this one was) were not locked in a cupboard; they were ranged upon shelves in the doctor's surgery.*

'There was no other person living in the house except Dr. Vidal and his wife. Dr. Vidal himself went out on his rounds most of every morning, from, I think, 10 o'clock onwards, and very often had to go out also in the afternoon and evening, and for one period, namely 19th to 22nd June, Mrs. Vidal was away altogether — she had occasion to go to London — so that for these three days there was only Dr. Vidal living in the house, and when he was out upon his rounds the defendant, during her hours of work — I am not exactly sure what they were — would be alone in the house, and she would therefore have full opportunity if so minded to take luminal tablets from the bottle. These tablets are sold to doctors in bottles holding no less than 1,000 — you can buy 500 or 1,000 — and he had at that time, I think, both sizes — certainly one or the other of those two sizes, and though he did not miss any, the bottle was in use; it had been used some way down before this happened, and you will readily understand that twenty, thirty or forty of these very small capsules would not make very much difference to a bottle which was somewhere round half full. *If the bottle had been quite full he might have noticed that as many had gone from the top, and if it had been nearly empty he might have noticed it had nearly got to the bottom, but being only half way you might think that he might not notice anything was missing.*

'Dr. Roche Lynch in due course made his report; he made his report, I think, on the 11th October, and on the 15th October Detective Sergeant Wild and a Police Inspector went from York to the house in Ampleforth where the defendant lived with her mother, and saw her in her mother's presence. They asked her: "Are you the mother of Colin Boulton?"; she said "Yes." She was then cautioned and told: "We are going to take you to York, where you will be charged with the murder of your son", and her reply was: "Why, he was never here." At York she was formally charged, and her answer was: "I am afraid I know nothing about it."

'She was searched and her house was searched and no drugs of this kind — no tablets of this kind — were found at all.'

Peroration

'Members of the Jury, those are the whole of the facts, which, with the assistance of my learned friend, I propose to

prove by witnesses, and if their evidence does prove to your
satisfaction that which I have outlined, then, in my
submission to you, unless there is some explanation which
I cannot give you, there would seem to be — and in my
submission there is — an almost overwhelming case
against this defendant.

'*All the facts, if unexplained, point in the same
direction; they point conclusively, in my submission, to
the fact that this little boy died of pheno-barbitone
poisoning; they point conclusively to the fact that only his
mother could have given it.*

'No doctor who had charge of this child at any stage ever
prescribed any pheno-barbitone, and the nurses who were in
charge of him will tell you that they never administered any
in hospital — I think you will be told it is kept under lock
and key in charge of the Sister in charge of the ward, and is,
of course, not issued except on doctors' orders.

'If those facts do satisfy you; if you are satisfied of the
truth of the evidence which will be called, in my submission
they make out almost an unanswerable case against this
defendant.'

There is just one further remark to be made about the
opening. If it is intended to say something (in advance) in
refutation of arguments likely to be raised by the defence,
the refutation should appear after the affirmative arguments
have set the case on firm foundation. In a defence or reply
the rule is the other way round: it is necessary to refute the
arguments of the other side and get them out of the way
before establishing a positive case.[104]

5 The speech in defence

Narrative is less important in a defence speech. The
introduction and peroration, however, may be very

[104]   This is Quintilian's advice: 'Si agimus, nostra
confirmanda sunt primum, tum quae nostris opponuntur,
refutanda; si respondemus prius incipiendum est a
refutatione.'

important as striking the right note to dispel prejudices
against the defendant. In the proof, as already noted, the first
thing is to refute the arguments on the other side, as until
these are removed they are an obstacle in the way of setting
up a positive case. Sometimes, indeed, the arguments for
the defence do not go beyond refutation.

A summary is given below of the speech of Cecil
Whiteley, K.C., in defence of Bywaters — a gallant
attempt in a hopeless task, and therefore the more
illuminating.[105] The substance of this case was that
Bywaters, a young sailor, and Mrs. Thompson, a married
woman, fell in love with one another. There was evidence
in Mrs. Thompson's letters (found in the possession of
Bywaters) that the two had plotted to poison Mr.
Thompson. Finally, Bywaters met Mr. and Mrs. Thompson
in the street one night and stabbed Thompson. The defence
was that there had been no premeditation, but that there had
been a sudden quarrel, and the blow was struck either in
self-defence or after provocation.

Introduction

(*to remove prejudice*)

1. Counsel's anxiety — not regarding the impartiality of
the jury but because the case had been embarrassed by
prejudicial evidence (i.e. the letters, the illicit amour) not
really connected with the essential facts.

Statement

2. Bywaters admits that his hand did the deed, but not
that it was murder.

Proof

Refutations

3. The evidence about the supposed plot to poison is
irrelevant and inconclusive. The letters are imaginative

[105] *Trial of Bywaters and Thompson,* pp. 105-112.

fiction. Their receipt by Bywaters does not prove that he agreed with them.

4. The knife does not prove premeditation. Such knives are commonly carried by sailors.

Positive arguments

5. The object of the meeting was to come to an arrangement (e.g. a divorce), not to murder.

6. Bywaters used the knife because he was provoked, or in self-defence, or in the heat of a sudden quarrel.

Peroration

7. Counsel challenged the prosecution to produce 'one stable piece of evidence' of an agreement to do harm to Thompson. Bywaters had drifted into a dishonourable entanglement, and had not the courage to break loose. 'All this is true', he says, 'but I am not an assassin.'

6 The reply

The object of the reply is to refute the arguments advanced by the defence, and to reinstate as strongly as possibly the advocate's own arguments, in the light of adverse attack. Thus the arguments are the important thing: the introduction and statement may be virtually non-existent, but the peroration may count, as giving a final impression. Below is the outline of the reply of Anthony Hawke, K.C., in the trial of Ley and Smith: his opening in the same case has already been quoted.

Proof

1st issue: the fact of murder.

1. Whatever conflict there may be regarding the ill-treatment of Mudie before his death, there is no doubt that he was strangled with a rope. The suggestion of suicide is ridiculous.

2nd issue: Ley's guilt.

2. His participation in the plot to bring Mudie to his house has been proved conclusively.

3. His jealous obsession is also proved.

4. His supposed alibi rests on his own word alone.

5. If he was at the house, is there any doubt that he was a party to the crime?

3rd issue: Smith's guilt.

6. The fact that he was seen making a reconnaissance of the chalk pit shatters his story.

7 Submission of no case to answer

A submission of no case to answer may be made, either in a criminal case or in a civil case tried by jury, at the conclusion of the case for the prosecution (or the plaintiff). In the event of the submissions being overruled, the defence goes on to present its case in the ordinary way.

In a civil case tried by a judge alone, the practice is to call upon counsel to elect whether he will stand on his submission or call evidence: he cannot do both.

A submission of no case rests either on a point of law or on the contention that the evidence is insufficient to support a verdict. Arguments on both these lines were fully explained in the last chapter, and further comment is unnecessary.[106]

[106] Similar observations apply to:
  (i) a motion to quash an indictment. (This must be made before the accused has pleaded to it.)
  (ii) an objection to the admissibility of evidence.

  Normally in these two cases a point of law is submitted quite briefly. Sometimes, however, the success or failure of a case may turn entirely on the admission of a disputed piece of evidence, as in the trial of G. J. Smith (the Brides in the Bath), where Smith was certain to be convicted if, under the rule of evidence relating to 'similar facts', the death of a whole series of previous 'wives' in their baths could be proved. In such a case, the objection to evidence will take the form of a full length speech, which may be the turning-point of the case.

8 Speech in mitigation

A speech in mitigation is really an appeal to the court to exercise favourably its discretion in passing sentence. Therefore, as in all cases where the exercise of a judicial discretion is in issue, the proper course is not to offer any arguments of a general character, but simply to draw the attention of the judge to those factors, leading up to or forming part of the offence, which would justify him in taking a lenient view. Thus attention may be drawn to natural human weaknesses which have led the prisoner into misfortune, not out of any wickedness, but almost in spite of himself.[107] This course can be taken even where the prisoner has a long record of convictions against him: for it may be shown that there was a lengthy period of time since the last one, that the prisoner was honestly trying to keep out of trouble, and that he would have succeeded but for a sudden temptation. Again, the fact that a technical offence was committed for a good motive may help. The essential in this sort of speech (which should as a rule be quite short) is to concentrate on the facts of the individual case and to avoid sentimental generalities which will probably irritate the judge.

---

[107] See Lord Birkenhead's well-known speech in mitigation of the bank clerk Goudie, quoted in part by Cassels J. in his lecture on *Advocacy*, pp. 28-29.

Chapter 10

General Strategy and Tactics

There is little or no *technique* in the conduct of a case as a whole: this is primarily an exercise of *practical judgment,* which has at its service the special techniques of speaking and of questioning witnesses. The intention of this chapter, therefore, is mainly to reiterate in a wider and more vivid way certain principles which have already been stressed in connection with the special techniques.

Such overall technique as there is displays a marked analogy to the principles of strategy and tactics in warfare: this is no accidental resemblance, for in both case there is a conflict between two opposing wills. Battles are fought in the quiet confines of courts of law, just as they are fought between contending armies, and it might be added that the counsel of today, if not the lineal descendant, is at least the ultimate successor of the champion in ordeal by battle. There is, of course, this limitation, that actions cannot be fought unscrupulously: in military tactics any device is legitimate to mystify and mislead the enemy, and attack him by surprise, but professional ethics does not allow any form of deceit in the law courts. With this qualification, however, the analogy is an illuminating one, and throws light on the fundamental factors in the conduct of a case.

The principles of strategy and tactics are these: (1) a firm base; (2) position and favourable conditions for battle; (3) striking power, consisting of men and weapons; (4) staying power — to which may be added the capacity to execute a retreat after a tactical reverse and to show resolute generalship in adversity.

The principles of legal strategy and tactics correspond closely, and will now be developed in detail

1 The foundation: knowledge of the case

Corresponding to the firm base of the military commander, the foundation of strategy in advocacy is a sure knowledge of the case — that is to say, of the version of the facts put forward by the party for whom the advocate appears. This should not be a knowledge of papers, but a picture of a living story. On this foundation rest fluency in speaking and ease in examination-in-chief: at the cross-examination stage, the advocate will know exactly what evidence he must challenge at all costs, and what can be reconciled, perhaps by a roundabout way, with his own story, and in cross-examining he will also manifest clearly his own version of events. Moreover, as soon as conflicting evidence is given, confusion arises and the inter-relation of details becomes obscure, giving rise to a fog of litigation which is very like the fog of war. The advocate will be deflected into irrelevancies and perhaps unwise admissions unless, in this fog, he keeps before him the clear picture which he had at the start.

The knowledge of facts includes understanding of technical questions. The problems arising in modern litigation involve such diverse topics as farming methods, electric wiring, the working of machines and human anatomy, and if any of these things are involved the advocate must inquire into the subject (with the help of expert witnesses) with sufficient thoroughness to appreciate what is being said, and to ask the right questions.

Two technical aids may be mentioned. The first is used by every competent advocate unless he has a phenomenal memory. This is to have a sheet containing a summary, in order of date, of the essential facts, or perhaps simply a list of dates. The second is not used so often in the courts, though it is a regular procedure in the civil service and at official conferences: this is to mark important letters with flags, so that they can be traced quickly when they are needed. (Where a point of law is to be argued, the pages in the law reports are similarly marked, and it is usual to hand in a list of authorities for the information of the court.)

2 Position and atmosphere

Position is sometimes deliberately sought after, for example by making admissions to obtain the right to begin, or by calling no evidence for the defence to obtain the right to the last word. In these cases there is always a corresponding sacrifice and it is a question of practical judgment whether the advantage of position outweighs this.

A matter of the highest importance is the selection of the issues on which a case is to be fought — always assuming that there is a choice. This again is a matter of practical judgment: Lord Birkenhead and Sir Patrick Hastings, two advocates of very different type, both showed a remarkable gift for selecting a central issue on which the case was to be fought. In the trial of Henry Fenton for fraudulent conversion,[108] shortly after the first World War, it

---

[108] Transcript lent to me by the courtesy of a friend. In his book *Cases in Court* (1949, pp. 109, 333), it is not surprising to find that Sir Patrick Hastings lays great stress on the selection of a single central point, and in fact he invariably followed this line of tactics. Such a course is certainly advisable before a jury, and possible in most libel actions and criminal defences: but there are many cases — especially big commercial actions — where it is

appeared that Fenton (a prominent wool magnate) had habitually used the bank account of his one-man company for his private purposes, and in this way had borrowed very large sums from the company. The wool slump followed, causing a depression in the value of the wool stocks, and the company went into liquidation, with the result that the security of the debenture-holders was endangered. Sir Patrick Hastings fought this complex case on a single issue: that the defendant's use of the company's money as his own had been quite open, that nobody challenged this because his ability to repay was unquestioned but for the unexpected slump, and that there was no dishonest intention. This strategy was successful: the defendant was acquitted, with the full concurrence of the judge. If the defence had been fought on several issues, the resulting confusion might easily have obscured the truth.

The creation of a favourable atmosphere enables the evidence and arguments to carry their maximum weight.[109] The main vehicle for creating atmosphere is the speeches, but the style and manner of examination-in-chief and cross-examination — especially the first questions in cross-examination — also assist.

3 Striking power

(i) Marshalling the arguments

The selection of the arguments and their arrangement in a convincing manner is the main thing in the preparation of

---

not possible to avoid a multiplicity of issues, and therefore Sir Patrick's advice cannot always be followed.

[109] Sir Patrick Hastings says (*op. cit.,* p. 47): 'It is difficult to over-estimate the effect of atmosphere at any trial at which a man's character is the matter of chief moment.' He returns to the point at pp. 335-337, and mentions (at p. 335) the importance of the first questions in cross-examination from this point of view.

the speeches. Weak arguments ought as a rule to be rejected, because if the judge or jury sees that certain arguments are weak he or they may come to the conclusion that the case as a whole is weak, if such arguments have to be introduced.

(ii) Marshalling the witnesses

Here, too, selection is important, because a weak witness may damage the case. A weak witness ought not, if possible, to be called first, or last, so as to give the first or last impression of the value of the evidence. Subject to this limitation, witnesses should be called, and documents produced, in the order best calculated to put forward the case in a clear and convincing light.

(iii) Surprise tactics

Surprise tactics — where the opportunity occurs — may be decisive: this would include a surprise argument, a surprise witness, and — most frequently — a surprise in cross-examination (as indicated in an earlier chapter).

4 Staying power and resolution

When a case develops adversely, the advocate needs staying power and resilience, the ability to wait coolly and without undue alarm until he is able to appreciate the situation thoroughly. A case which appears to be hopeless may give an unexpected turn in the other direction, or the opposite party, or one of his witnesses, may make a foolish slip: resilience ensures that the opening can be seized and turned to advantage, so that perhaps victory is snatched from the jaws of defeat.

At other times the advocate may be satisfied that, with the weight of evidence produced against him, he is certain to lose: he must then make a quick decision and seek honourable terms before he is forced to unconditional surrender.

However, there are occasions (as in a criminal trial) where terms are impossible. The only course then open to the advocate is to go on arguing and cross-examining strongly until the end: so, like a resolute general, overcome in spite of his generalship by forces beyond his control, he will go down fighting.

Chapter 11

Learning the Techniques

The preceding chapters have analysed the various techniques of advocacy. In this chapter — which has been specially written for the new edition — some ideas are advanced for *learning* these techniques.

1 The techniques of questioning

There is no need to add anything to what was said about the preparation of speeches, whether they are narratives of fact or arguments of law. The traditional moots in the Inns of Court and in law students' societies give excellent practice in arguing law; and any reasonably educated and intelligent person should be able to prepare an orderly narrative of fact.

The difficult thing is the technique of asking questions. Now cross-examination always seems mysterious, and in the book perhaps an excessive spotlight is thrown on it. But the really important thing, the key skill, is examination-in-chief.

Anyone who has acquired the ability to bring out a story—

(a)   in the right order
(b)   without missing a point
(c)   by short, simple questions

(d)   which do not *lead* the witness by suggesting the answer

has made himself a thoroughly competent advocate. Everything else will follow. Yet some lawyers, in spite of long experience, have never acquired these skills. Long, muddled verbose questions are common.

Frankly, the traditional method of 'Sit by Aggie and see what she does' is not good enough. In my view it is worth putting in hard work at the start of one's career: this requires deliberate 'drills' or exercises, just as one needs to learn the right way of using a tennis racket or golf club or compass or performing a high jump or for that matter solving differential equations or multiplying matrices. You do not acquire techniques, as you acquire knowledge, just by reading about them.

2 Drills for learning

The author has suggested to numerous beginners at the bar that they should practice on printed narratives packed with detail such as the short stories of Sherlock Holmes. These lend themselves to steady practice better than proofs in briefs, some of which may give good practice while others do not.

The four points mentioned above should at first be practised *one at a time,* as it is too much to cope with them all together.

First: to frame questions so that they do not 'lead'. This is fairly familiar, because traditionally it is the one thing pupils have been told to master. There are two ways of doing it. One is to leave the key idea completely blank. *e.g.*

Did you notice his hair?
What colour was it?

The other which is less satisfactory, is to put it in the alternative:

Was his hair light or dark?

Sometimes this cannot be avoided, but the other way is preferable. The 'x or y' question often has a slant towards one alternative. 'Did he tell you about the buried gold or not?' would be blatant leading. The 'what was it' question ("Did he give you any new information?') never leads.

Second: to keep the question short and simple. Sadly, many have never mastered this. Some eminent persons asked questions which were always a mile long. This is where practice with printed narratives is valuable. Also it will be found that keeping questions short and not cramming too much into them at once helps to frame 'non-leading' questions; further, that a 'short-question' skill is enormously valuable in cross-examination.

The other two skills — getting things in the right order and bringing out every detail — also work in together. But the first step is to get the main events or topics in the right order: then, within each of them, bring out even tiny details Printed stories are particularly helpful at this stage. They are in the right order already, but contain a lot of detail.

3 Witnesses' proofs

The next stage is to turn to witnesses' proofs. These are often higgledly-piggledy (which is why they are not the best starting material). The first task is to get them in the right order. Decide which are the *main* topics — five or six probably unless it is a long Chancery or commercial or patent case where the proof is as big as a book. Enclose each main topic in a red line — which will often require loops into other paragraphs or into afterthoughts added at the end. In the margin against the top of each topic put a big number in a ring: (1). Then divide the topic into sub-topics (a), (b), (c) etc. Then divide these into details (i), (ii), (iii). If this subdivision is not enough, you have made your main topic too big. *Unwanted* material should be crossed out lightly (not obliterated) so that you do not waste time.

In practising examination-in-chief with such a proof, you must finish (1) before you go on to (2); within (1) finish (a) before you go on to (b), and within (a) bring out (i), (ii), and (iii) in order. You can tick off each item as it is disposed of.

4 Taking statements

Much of what is said above about examination-in-chief applies equally to the preliminary taking of statements. In particular questions should be short and simple; long complex questions confuse the witness. It is also better not to 'lead' the witness when he first tells his story. Most people are 'suggestible' and tend to give the answer which they think is wanted. But it is usually hopeless to get the first statement in the right order. It is best to skim through the story quickly, taking only brief notes, then take it in detail in the right order.

5 Cross-examination

In retrospect, much of the treatment of cross-examination in the first edition of this book was out of balance — though none of it was actually wrong — because of the excessive emphasis on what was called 'massive confrontation' as exemplified by the Oscar Wilde libel case. Wilde was a successful and witty dramatist in the 1880s. The libel was that he was 'posing as a sodomite' and massive evidence was produced that he did a great deal more than 'posing'. This sort of case is brought into the limelight by adulatory books on successful advocates, and the author was unduly impressed by Marjoribanks' life of Carson. But such cases are 'freak' cases, usually libels on famous characters whose whole life is brought up against them after exhaustive inquiries by detectives. In reality, 'massive confrontation' is not a separate technique, but simply an extreme example of 'firm insinuation'. So far as the Wilde case is concerned, he did not have a ghost of a chance with the mass of evidence built up against him.

So there are only two techniques in cross-examination: probing and insinuation.

Now *probing* is simply asking questions of detail about what the witness has said — or left unsaid. *Insinuation* is asking him to agree to some positive suggestion (though when counsel aggressively uses the clichés 'I suggest to you', 'I put it to you', his technique is lacking in subtlety).

Probing therefore simply needs the skill of asking short questions on points of detail which (if the above suggestions are followed) has already been acquired in examination in chief.

Insinuation takes two very different forms: firm, or gentle. It is firm insinuation when the facts have been so clearly proved in the case or are so incontrovertible that — if put to the witness carefully, point by point — they cannot be denied. Usually this is combined with a process of logical deduction in which the facts, taken in the right order, lead to a damaging conclusion, and the important thing is the marshalling of the facts in the right order, closing every loophole. A common example is the cross-examination of the defendant in a criminal case. Though such cross-examinations are often called 'brilliant', this is usually excessive praise. They can certainly be done badly, and leave loose ends. But to do them competently does not require great ingenuity, because the defendant is a 'sitting duck'. (The Wilde case was an example of this: with the accumulated evidence all Carson had to do was to marshall his facts in the right order and 'pin him down'.) What such cases do require is great attention to detail, pinning down the witness point by point so that he cannot wriggle out of the conclusion to which they lead.

Of course, all insinuation is by leading questions. But the other skills which should have been practised for examination-in-chief — short questions, in the right order, every detail — are all precisely in point.

Gentle insinuation is where you do not know what is going to come out, so you have to approach the critical questions very gradually, feeling your way little by little. The old anecdote books about advocacy used to warn about the 'dangerous' or 'unnecessary' question which has been put a little too soon and produces a catastrophic answer. When to stop has to be a matter of judgment. But the ability to frame very short questions and not ask too much at once is essential. An advocate who has great charm, like Norman Birkett, excels in this technique.

Any given cross-examination will alternate all the time between these three modes. A probing question may be followed by a gentle insinuation and that in turn by a sudden pounce of firm insinuation.

Incredible as it may seem, some advocates prepare detailed questions for cross-examination, but this cannot often work successfully. It is useful, however, to have a general *schema* — an outline of main topics and sub-topics to be covered, the mirror image of the analysis of a proof — so that the objects you hope to achieve are kept in view.

Normally the aim of cross-examination is to get at the truth, even from an unwilling witness. But it can be used in a different way if the evidence is believed to be false and bogus (it is better not to speak of *lying* witnesses — people have an extraordinary ability to convince themselves by wishful thinking). Probing may then be used to 'lead on' the witness to add detail after detail until the story becomes more and more improbable and then an insinuation put (often introduced by a sardonic 'I suppose') which brings out its absurdity. Even an honest and independent witness is unwilling to admit that he was mistaken, and rather than retract he will embroider his story to justify himself, without any conscious intent to lie.

So the same basic skills learnt in examination-in-chief will also greatly facilitate cross-examination. They are, of course, essentially skills to give ease and facility in the use of words and the marshalling of facts. Their application in examination-in-chief is straightforward. To deploy them in cross-examination requires a sense of tactics and judgment. These cannot be learnt, but there is no mystery about them. Tactics is simply flexibility in choosing the means to effect the object in view. Judgment is mainly a matter of degree and timing. A *schema* as indicated above will keep the aims of the cross-examination in view — assuming it is a major witness — and therefore be a guide to tactics.